Using Sports for Reading and Writing Activities:

Elementary and Middle School Years

A Fun with Reading Book

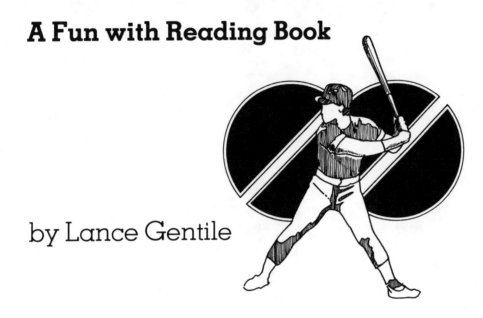

by Lance Gentile

ORYX PRESS
1983

The rare Arabian Oryx is believed to have inspired the myth of the unicorn. At that time several groups of international conservationists arranged to have 9 animals sent to the Phoenix Zoo to be the nucleus of a captive breeding herd. Today the Oryx population is over 400 and herds have been returned to reserves in Israel, Jordan, and Oman.

Library of Congress Cataloging in Publication Data

Gentile, Lance M., 1940–
   Using sports for reading and writing activities.

   Bibliography: p.
   1. Language arts.   2. Sports—Addresses, essays, lectures.   I. Title.
LB1576.G38   420'.07'12   82-6322
ISBN 0-89774-023-8   AACR2

*This book is dedicated to
my mother, Mary A. Gentile;
my father, Alfonso F. Gentile;
and Merna M. McMillan.
They showed me the benefits of
reading and writing
and always encouraged my participation
in sports.*

Contents

Acknowledgments

Using Sports for Reading and Writing Activities: Elementary and Middle School Years, has occupied a good portion of my time for the past 5 years. I would like to thank my graduate students at Oregon State University, Pan American University, and North Texas State University for all the help they rendered me during this period. In particular, special thanks to Betty Ackerman, Becky Adams, Stan Diers, Sharon Dodge, Bronnie Helton, Patrice Lamb, Barbara Scott, and Jennifer Thornhill, who assisted me in developing the activities for this book. Additional thanks are in order to Roy A. Robinson for helping me develop the annotated bibliography. Thanks and sincere appreciation to my editors Sam Mongeau and Susan Slesinger for their thorough and expert attention to detail, and to Linda Archer and Linda Vespa for their excellent production work. A special thanks to Phyllis Steckler for believing in this book and contracting to publish it. Finally, thanks to my secretary, Carol Schrader, for the excellent job of typing the final manuscript.

I wish to recognize the following individuals as people who have contributed to my appreciation of reading and thinking during athletic competition:

Bruce, Eric, Mike, and Ken Gentile
Donald MacDonald
James Corcoran
Mickey Wittman
Ted Uhaelander
Jim Fitzgerald
Hank Zurretti
Bruce Fowland
Bob Theard
Mike Wilson
Jim Buzewski
George Rowan
Al George
David Ellison

Bob Micus
Jay Shutt
John Leslie
Pat McCary
Eldon Rouse
Neil Jordan
Fred Holdsworth
Lloyd Houden
Bill McElroy
Ray Null
Arnold Habig
Jack Vincent
Bill Chestnut
Vince Pacent
Jack Gurney

Tom Pomarolli
Bud Jones
Tom Baluk
John Baluk
Tom Wade
Bob Morrison
Sean Whalen
Steve Stockdale
John Lehner
Keith DesJardais
Stan Johnson
Frank Ryan
John Ferguson
Dale Matson
William V. Mixie

and
In Memory Of:

Ed Buote
Gary Halverson

Ted Linstruth
Paul Gentile

Harry Wertz
Ray Kowalski

Reading and Writing

In the education of children there is nothing like alluring the appetites and affection; otherwise you make so many asses laden with books.

—Montaigne, 1533–1592

This workbook contains a wide variety of material directed at teaching and learning in the areas of word recognition, vocabulary, comprehension, and study skills by providing parents, teachers, and students with reading and writing activities using sports as a backdrop.

The Need to Read   Generally, reading affects our perceptions in 2 ways. The first definition concerns the interpretation of various nonprint signs, symbols, gestures, signals, or pictorial illustrations. We speak of the Native American's uncanny ability to "read" impressions in the dirt or messages rising through the air in the form of smoke puffs; a CB operator "reads" his "good buddy" loud and clear; doctors "read" x-rays and symptoms of various diseases; a quarterback "reads" an opponent's defensive alignment; the psychologist "reads" body language; backpackers "read" compasses; sailors "read" semaphores or the weather; the deaf "read" lips, etc.

Secondly, reading refers to an individual's capacity to recognize graphic symbols or written words and understand, explain, or critique ideas in print. It considers a person's ability to recall or paraphrase an author's direct and implied meanings.

Stated specifically: Reading requires the active involvement of the intellect. As the athlete uses calisthenics to stimulate his/her muscle tone and strength, the reader uses the process of reading to stimulate the perceptive and cognitive areas of the mind.

The demands of business, job, or school force us to read obligatory information to accomplish a task. This type of reading requires the ability to make reports, take tests, follow directions, and develop other specific skills.

We also read for enjoyment and personal growth as we explore new ideas. Reading is a form of contemplation whose purpose is to affect learning or provide spiritual and emotional satisfaction. This type of reading precludes duty or obligation and occurs anywhere, anytime. Both kinds of reading are essential in today's world: the first for job or school success; the second for entertainment, joy, personal fulfillment and stimulation, or escape from some of the drudgery and tedium of everyday life.

It appears, unfortunately, that much of what goes on in traditional reading instruction is skill development and preparation rather than the actual process of reading. Teachers have even been heard to say, "All right, let's put away our books now, it's time for reading." Through this distorted lens, it is small wonder that many students view reading as monotonous, tiresome drill.

This workbook provides an alternative to the drudgery of drill by presenting activities in which the sports-oriented student may employ his/her experience directly and become an active participant in the reading process.

When will students learn to read or choose to read? The answer to this question is simple. Students will learn to read or choose to read when it makes sense to do so. However, interestingly enough, they can only become adept at reading *by reading!* Unfortunately much of what goes on with respect to reading in school too often ignores youngsters' "natural cravings to be mentally alive," overlooks their passions or "appetites," and, by so doing, reduces reading to a wearisome process whose sole purpose is the recall, memorization, and recitation of uninteresting and disjointed information. Consequently, many children never grasp the duality reading plays in their emotional and intellectual development.

These youngsters never equate reading with art or with what Malcolm X (1965) referred to in his autobiography as an inherent "drive to read." The author observed:

> I have often reflected upon the new vistas reading opened to me. I knew right there in prison reading had changed forever the course of my life. As I see it today, the ability to read awoke inside me some long dormant craving to be mentally alive. I certainly wasn't seeking any degree, the way a college confers a status symbol upon its students. Not long ago, an English writer telephoned me from London, asking questions. One was, 'What's your alma mater?' I told him, 'Books.' (p. 179).

How Reading and Writing Relate

Reading maketh a full man, conference a ready man, and writing an exact man.
—*Francis Bacon, 1560–1626*

Writing is much more than jotting letters and words on paper. Writers must be motivated to express something in a particular way. Essentially, writing is a unique conversation imprinted on paper. A good author chooses the correct words and uses them to kindle a thoughtful/emotional response of the reader.

Reading requires the interpretation of symbols; writing involves creating the symbols. While distinctions exist between the 2 processes, reading and writing are basically indivisible and mutually supportive. As a person's writing improves so does his/her reading and, generally, the opposite is true.

Many very young children develop a spontaneous love of using crayons, paintbrushes, and pencils to illustrate their feelings or impressions. Later, they become enamored of using language to transcribe "messages" to parents, relatives, or friends. This continues through kindergarten and first grade, where children are encouraged to write their favorite words and phrases or make up stories based on real or imaginary events. However, in the second and third grades, children begin the task of learning to write correctly. Writing becomes something they have to do as a portion of their academic training, which requires precise elements of form and style.

However, children's acquisition of handwriting skills, which allows them to form letters and words legibly and correctly, is only a first step. Thereafter, children must also learn to write their ideas, using language that communicates their thoughts and feelings. This is a very delicate period in their development. If *too* much emphasis is placed on "correct" handwriting, spelling, or grammar, many children become inhibited toward writing and fear making mistakes. In many instances, they lose the intellectual/ emotional freedoms that prompted their earlier expression. Furthermore, since what has been written is essentially pure self-expression, criticism that stresses form (e.g., grammar and handwriting) over function (e.g., creative, joyous, self-expression) can severely damage youngsters' eagerness and willingness to develop their writing.

Because of these constraints many children soon perceive writing as a chore and much of their early fascination with it is destroyed. For the remainder of these youngsters' school lives, writing is by and large a mandated, structured, impersonal, and graded activity.

Most teachers are aware that writing, like reading, requires practice if youngsters are to become proficient. Students must devote ample time and energy to developing these skills if they are to acquire the literary strengths that will allow them smooth passage through the grades.

Writing as a duty is probably unavoidable insofar as all of us must attend school for a specified period, and "scholarship" is one factor that earmarks our educational progress. There is a distinct difference, however, between writing in this manner and writing enthusiastically and creatively. A Chinese philosopher (1974, pp. 388–389) made a clear statement in this regard:

> A "scholar's" writing consists of borrowings from other scholars, and the more authorities and sources he quotes, the more of a "scholar" he appears. A thinker's writing consists of borrowings from ideas in his own intestines, and the greater thinker a man is, the more he depends on his own intestinal juice. A scholar is like a raven feeding its young that spits out what it has eaten from the mouth. A thinker is like a silkworm which gives us not mulberry leaves, but silk.
>
> —*Lin Yutang*

Just as *real* reading involves intense thinking on the part of a reader, *real* writing makes the same demands on a writer. Although most of us mimic the writing of scholars, only a few of us ever apply ourselves to becoming writers. Writing for pleasure is something most people are capable of doing. However, the development of a person's writing for creative, meaningful self-expression is by and large also a matter of hard work and devoted practice. Again, as with reading, the more one writes, the better writer s/he becomes.

Reading, Writing, and Other Media

In recent times, parents and teachers have been drenched by reports concerning "Why Johnny and Joanie Can't Read or Write." Frequently, it is these people who receive the blame when students fail to acquire the basic skills; are unmotivated to participate in reading and writing activities; or casually dismiss literary pursuits as being the unmeaningful, obligatory, and rather bothersome business of school.

At a time when our youth identify strongly with television, motion pictures, radio, records, and electronic games, it is extremely difficult to argue for the unique rewards and advantages of effective reading and writing.

There can be no question that the media have made a great impact on most people's lives in this country. Ironically, however, the demands for improved reading and writing skills in the professional world, and throughout business or industry, have in-

"Mrs. Horton, could you stop by school today?"

creased markedly during the past 10–15 years. Entrance requirements over this same period for leading high schools and universities (not to mention private kindergartens) have stiffened as well. We are living in an age when professional, vocational, technological, industrial, and educational success can be directly affected by an individual's ability to use reading and writing as a means of expressing ideas. The most rapidly spreading technology of our time, computers, demands competent readers and writers.

While many media may be used to dispense information as effectively as books or written material, "information dumping" is not the distinguishing function of reading and writing. Many people have come to believe that information—facts, facts, and more facts—is all there is to knowledge. Apart from communicating information, reading and writing constitute 2 specific ways to develop the language/thought processes. They are exceptional in that they offer means to create, introduce, explore, expand, or critique ideas, and to generate *new experiences*.

"Information dumping" is a secondary purpose for reading and writing. There are other technologies to replace literacy in this regard, but other media cannot substitute for the journey or "trip" one realizes while reading or writing. They can never stand in lieu of the growth and excitement the individual experiences when reading or developing a written expression of true personal meaning. Books or written materials and readers or authors grow together. Carl Sandburg described the impact of reading on the young Abraham Lincoln saying, "It seemed that Abe made books tell him more than they told other people."

Alternate media might better be seen as different tools for presenting information to help resolve different problems. These technologies are not, however, alternatives to reading and writing. No other medium allows the users as much control as reading or writing does. This is true for 2 reasons:

1. The reader or writer has complete control over time. When writing or reading prose and poetry, the writer or reader has total control over the organization and presentation of ideas as well as the rate at which these thoughts are written or processed. Consequently, written text offers the writer or reader enormous power or absolute control over speeding up and slowing down the flow of ideas. The writer or reader may also opt to go back and rewrite, reread, or skip over portions of the text and decide upon the sequence for expressing or absorbing ideas. Moreover, other media lack something only print can provide: time to contemplate. No matter how many ideas might be developed in a TV show or movie, they can only become ours when we reflect on them, and that requires time, effort, and practice. Thus, reading and writing compel the individual to function in a unique manner.

> Sometimes when I can't go to sleep at night I see a family of the future. Dressed in three-tone shorts-and-shirt sets of disposable papersilk, they sit before the television wall of their apartment, only their eyes moving. After I've looked for awhile, I always see—otherwise I'd die—a pigheaded soul in the corner with a book; only his eyes are moving, but in them is a different look. —*Randall Jarrell*

2. The reader or writer has extensive control over the material. In variance to television, radio, motion pictures, or records, the reader or writer has an infinite number of choices when it comes to determining what s/he will read or write. Libraries and bookstores are jammed with a wide range of written materials detailing the pros and cons of issues or ideas and covering a wide variety of topics. However, when one turns on the TV or watches a movie, s/he is "programed" or controlled by a limited number of alternatives. Furthermore, there are relatively few television or motion picture producers, directors, and screenwriters, and these people decide what the public will see. They exert great command over what the viewer experiences. For this reason, books and written materials, in their vast abundance, written from a wide range of perspectives, may be our greatest remedy against a "mindless orthodoxy" and the monitoring or total control of human beings by those of invidious or treacherous intentions.

How Do Reading and Writing Compare with Sports?

A sport is usually an activity that is performed for pleasure, excitement, or recreation, so in a large sense, reading and writing are "sports." Like other sports, they also require mastery of fundamental skills, sufficient practice, a balanced series of daily exercises, and a lifetime of development. In addition, readers and writers need good models or demonstrators—coaches—to become successful, active participants rather than passive spectators. The following diagram shows the proximity of these areas:

SPORTS ◄───────────────► READING & WRITING

1. Good coaches/teachers and responsive players/students.
2. Structured and consistent teaching methods.
3. Sequential mastery of fundamental skills.
4. Appropriate intellectual and emotional responses.
5. A willingness and enthusiasm among players/students to compete with themselves and others for higher levels of achievement.
6. Continuous motivation and reinforcement.
7. An abundance of self-discipline, perseverance, and practice.

Since the dawn of Western Civilization, educators have recognized the crucial relationship that exists between physical activity and learning. Plato placed gymnastics at the highest level for training his philosopher-king. Spinoza claimed, "Teach the body to do many things; this will help you perfect the mind and come to the intellectual level of thought."

Currently, sports is a popular field of study because of expanded leisure, the growth of a national interest in physical fitness, and the media's broad coverage and glorification of athletes and athletics.

For many young people, who are motivated by sports and have had ample vicarious and *real-life* experiences in sporting activities, sports as subject matter *makes sense*. It provides a vehicle to stimulate not only those who are uninterested in "academic" pursuits or unmotivated to read or write, but can be used to strengthen the abilities of good students and enthusiastic readers and writers as well.

Using Sports to Develop Students' Critical Reading and Writing Skills

The direct connection with sport should not be hard to detect; sport contributes to an improvement in our quality of life in a unique manner. It builds self-reliance and brings the family and community together in social harmony. Sport is the counterpoint to the pressures of life and sometimes it seems a sane point in a world becoming increasingly structured and limited by economics, national boundaries, political ideologies, religion, and race. Sport remains a free expression of personal creativity, a universal means of communication and an expression of physical joy.
—*Justice Beattie—Chair, New Zealand Sports Foundation*

A slight revision of Mr. Beattie's last statement provides greater comparisons among reading, writing, and sports: "Reading and writing remain free expressions of personal creativity, they are universal means of communication and expressions of intellectual joy." These are the ideal purposes for reading and writing and are realized when students select or are introduced to reading materials or writing activities whose content and objectives reflect their "tastes" and "appetites." Under these circumstances reading and writing cannot be inappropriate or distasteful for anyone.

While reading, writing, and sports share many elements, one notable contradiction exists among them. In sports, the majority of young people are drawn to perform, dedicated to practice or compete, and strive for self-improvement or recognition. But many youngsters never demonstrate equal fervor when it comes to developing themselves as readers and writers. There are several reasons for this dilemma, yet the following 3 are most significant:

1. Not uncommonly, reading and writing are taught as discreet, skill-oriented subjects throughout the elementary grades. Most youngsters who learn to read and write well do so despite years of repetitious drill or workbook "fill-in-the-blank" activities. After several years' exposure to this kind of instruction, many see reading and writing as boring and turn to other features of the curriculum, e.g., sports, music, art, shop, etc., for purposes of self-fulfillment. For many students, this attitude remains unchanged throughout their high school years and beyond.

2. Unlike the Greeks and Romans or some present-day European and Asian societies, American society has tended to separate the development of the mind and body in its educational approach. Consequently, a clear and detrimental distinction between "intellectuals" and "jocks" is made very early in youngsters' lives.

3. In America athleticism is cherished. Reggie Jackson, the star baseball player, recently remarked, "Fifty years ago it was Bogart and Cagney. Twenty-five years ago it was Elvis Presley and Chubby Checker. Now it's the age of the athlete." Many of our sports figures are worshipped and receive incomparable recognition and rewards for their "work." Apart from a few selected writers, there is no equivalent admiration or payment accorded those Americans who distinguish themselves through reading and writing achievements. In fact, the "bookworm" or "egghead" (2 rather contemptible sobriquets) is more likely to be seen by some as unathletic or puerile and, thus, undeserving of approval.

One of the most frustrating problems faced by teachers at all levels is not so much a student's inability to read or write, but his/her helplessness or resistance toward thinking deeply about what s/he has read and written. Teachers claim most of their students can "bark" at print or write words and sentences, but they are ill-equipped or ill-disposed to interpret or compose ideas critically. Frequently, they cannot interpret an author's meanings and struggle to write logically, forcefully, creatively, and cohesively. The failure to generate a "cognitive commerce" with the written page is perhaps the primary reason many students never acquire a sense of purpose for reading and writing.

There is a general agreement among educators that *real* reading and writing involves a rather complex interactive thinking/questioning process. Moreover, critical reading and writing are by-products of concentration, which is the outgrowth of an arousal of interest on the reader or writer's part. This level of functioning can be expected to occur only when the material or activities "suit" an individual and there is an accompanying positive, emotional reaction to whatever is read or written. If what a person reads or writes is "unsuitable," lacks meaning, or is uninteresting, any measurable benefit related to the time spent in the process will be short-lived or insignificant. In this respect, reading and writing are no different than sports. When a reader, writer, or athlete performs unemotionally or impassively, the results are predictably feeble and uninspiring.

Additionally, readers and writers must have certain vicarious experiences that provide a foundation for them to think critically. Students can and will think critically about something that intersects with their knowledge, background of experience, or level of interest. The following diagram illustrates the interrelated factors that lead to a reader or writer's critical thinking:

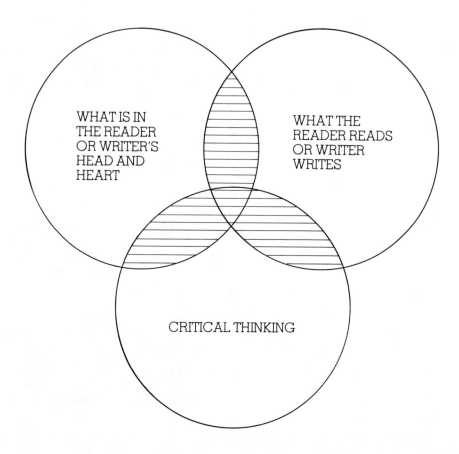

WHAT IS IN
THE READER
OR WRITER'S
HEAD AND
HEART

WHAT THE
READER READS
OR WRITER
WRITES

CRITICAL THINKING

Students develop critical thinking skills when they accept and resolve certain challenges posed by various reading material or writing assignments. Whenever what they read or write introduces new challenges that create just the right amount of tension to encourage them to use what they already know, critical thinking will take place. Unsuccessful student readers or writers are those who cannot, or do not, make the appropriate intellectual and emotional adjustments during their literary activities and thus fail to develop new thought patterns to meet ever increasing needs and challenges in school. It is not surprising, therefore, to find that students who lack these essential antecedents resist or have great difficulty thinking about, understanding, or valuing their reading and writing assignments. In sum, frequently the material or activity makes no sense to them.

Unfortunately, the current thrust of research in reading and writing tends to dismiss the unquantifiable psychodynamic variables of "what is in the reader or writer's head and heart," and by doing so dehumanizes the reading and writing processes. This perpetuates the image of a reader or writer as a computer, and encourages the use of instructional approaches and materials that become mechanical, predictable, and ritualistic.

The meaningless interaction between many students and books, and their failure to produce consummate ideas, opinions, or sentiments when they write may account for why so many of them are quick to answer, "it's boring," when asked why they do not like a certain subject. Many other factors, such as the absence of teacher enthusiasm, adversive peer influence, or the negative attitudes of significant others (family members, etc.), may account for the apathy or disdain some students bear toward reading and writing. But, in essence, many of these young people are stung, bewildered, bored, and angered by the prospects of having to read and write about things that do not speak personally to them and which they perceive as providing little or no intrinsic or extrinsic reward. Recently I asked one student why she had not read a 15-page homework assignment in history and written out the answers to several questions related to the reading. She responded matter-of-factly: "We ain't never gonna need this stuff!"

Often, there are 2 reasons for this dilemma:

1. Many students lack the language experiences to interact vigorously and knowledgeably with what they must read and write about in the various academic content areas. Often, teachers overlook or ignore these deficits and make no adjustments in their teaching to compensate for them. Their instruction lacks any use of concrete introductory examples of those facets of language (spelling or vocabulary) with which students may be unfamiliar.

2. As I pointed out previously, many students lack the vicarious or actual experiences that allow them to read certain materials

insightfully or to write critically. Many teachers also overlook or ignore these limitations and fail to adjust their teaching to compensate for them. Consequently, their instructional approach does not relate new terms, ideas, information, or learning experiences to students' lives by placing them in a context with which most youngsters can identify, value, and discover personal meanings.

For many young people reading, writing, and sports comprise one very meaningful context. While various topics can be motivating to those students, probably no single subject matter other than sports has more potential to capture their full imagination and interest. At first this may seem like an overblown statement, but upon closer consideration, it is apparent that sports contains all the vital elements that make life interesting and exciting. Everyday the features of human drama, tragedy, comedy, challenge, perseverance, romance, victory, and defeat are acted out in a myriad of sporting events around the world. These accounts are documented and chronicled in newspapers, magazines, and books and are shown to millions of television viewers.

Parents and teachers working to expand students' reading and writing skills will discover that, by involving them in instructional activities that make use of published sports materials, they establish a provocative climate in which to learn. Many young people have developed a large store of language as well as real-life and vicarious experiences in sports that parents or teachers can use as a springboard to further learning. These youngsters have not only actively participated in sports but have spend a considerable number of hours watching live and televised sports contests. They have listened to broadcasters, players, or performers describe the action or circumstances surrounding various games and events. In doing so they have acquired a host of related vocabulary and ideas.

Many students have also accumulated an abundance of knowledge and statistics concerning the history of sports, sports figures, rules, strategies, events, teams, etc. *They are motivated to apply or demonstrate what they know and want to learn more!* For this reason, parents and teachers can employ sports-related reading and writing exercises as powerfully effective means of strengthening students' critical reading and writing abilities. These include sports magazines, the sports sections of newspapers, biographies of sports heroes, publications containing sports quotes, trivia, superstition, poetry, and humor. Such material can be adapted to provide young people the following specific learning experiences that will contribute heavily to their critical reading and writing skills:

1. Opportunities that motivate students to become active readers and writers instead of passive word callers or copiers.

2. Opportunities for vocabulary and language enrichment.

3. Opportunities to perform critical reading and writing skills, e.g., distinguish between fact and opinion or cause and effect; locate likenesses and differences; identify main ideas, sequence of events, or character traits; critique an author's premise for strengths or weaknesses, and act as an author to create a clear, interesting piece of writing for someone else to read.

4. Opportunities to collect and organize data, do inductive and deductive thinking, stimulate interpretive or creative thinking, and introduce a variety of situations that require problem solving operations.

5. Opportunities to practice, apply, and develop general reading and writing skills in a sports context that transfer to school-based academic subjects.

A wide variety of examples for parents' and teachers' use that help accomplish these aims and employ the above listed sports materials appear in Section 3. These have been created for students in the elementary and middle school grades.

Parents and Teachers as Models of Literacy

> You are the bows from which your children as living arrows are sent forth.
>
> —*Kahlil Gibran, 1883–1931*

Parents and teachers are in the unique position of having great influence on the behavior of young people. Generally, they are models for youngsters and it is not uncommon to hear remarks like, "she takes after her mother in that respect" or "he worships his teacher."

> Such identifications, particularly in the form of "hero worship," may play an important role in shaping the personality development of a child, who strives to be like his hero in dress and manner. He shapes his own values after those of his hero.
>
> —*J. C. Coleman*

The powerful effects of modeling are explained in the quote above (1964, p. 103). Initially, many youngsters assign importance and meaning to an activity by virtue of *who* does it rather than on what is being done. Gradually, they develop an implicit joy for doing certain things, but this usually follows an explicit desire and drive to please or emulate those they admire or love.

When parents and teachers emphasize the need to read, underscore literary or academic achievement as well as athletic performance, and *read* and *write* themselves, young people are drawn to these endeavors. By making reading and writing important for students and showing them how these processes positively affect their own thinking and behavior, parents and teachers become strong models of literacy.

Today there is a tendency for parents to blame teachers and vice versa for the lack of interest students show in developing reading and writing skills. In truth, the home and school share a joint responsibility for helping young people identify with and develop a sense of meaning or worth for reading and writing. When parents and teachers unite in this effort, students cannot help but see the importance of acquiring these skills.

However, if children do not see their parents and teachers reading or writing and *benefiting* from doing so, it is improbable that they will attach great value or purpose to these pursuits. By adhering to the following prescription on a day-to-day basis, parents and teachers can provide sound purposes for reading and writing and present themselves as healthy models of literacy.

INSTRUCTIONAL PREREQUISITES FOR GROWTH AND DEVELOPMENT—THE PARENT'S AND TEACHER'S ROLES

1. Allow youngsters uninterrupted time to read and write each day. Research shows that those students experiencing the most difficulty in reading and writing actually have the least amount of time to practice at home or in school. While many parents and teachers stress mastery of fundamental skills, the opportunity for students to read books, magazines, or newspapers without interference is frequently omitted or overlooked.

2. Begin reading to youngsters every day. Many parents and teachers are comfortable doing this with students in the early grades, but they should continue doing so for students in middle, junior high, and high school as a means of developing and fostering interest in different subject areas. This helps kindle young people's imaginations and provides sorely needed practice in listening.

3. Converse with youngsters as an integral part of each day's training. Some time should be made for purposes of discussing students' problems, concerns, dreams, hopes, and expectations. Many of these discussions can form the basis for reading and

writing activities. They help trigger youngsters' enthusiasm for exploring ideas with greater intensity.

4. Do not fall prey to students' complaints or resistance to reading and writing activities. Remember that at first these activities will cause some unrest among many youngsters who have had a history of reading or writing difficulties. However, in time, students will come to appreciate the rewards of literary enterprise through the efforts of concerned, inquisitive parents and teachers who structure diverse and provocative literary experiences.

5. Expect students to write something every day. These activities or assignments may include poetry as well as prose, editorial comments regarding newspaper articles, satire, political or religious statements, letters, humorous accounts, and journal or diary notations.

Reading, Writing, and Sports for Everyone

The surge of interest throughout this country in sports and physical fitness is not confined to males, as it once may have been. Women of all ages, lured to arenas, pools, fields of every description, jogging lanes, or gymnasiums by Title IX of the Educational Amendments Act (1972), are more staunch zealots than the men. This is evidenced by their record number of participants in athletics.

- Eight years ago, fewer than 300,000 high school girls participated in interscholastic sports. This year the number will be close to 2 million—nearly a sevenfold increase.
- The Association for Intercollegiate Athletics for Women (AIAW), formed just 7 years ago, today has 825 active member schools— more than its male counterpart, the National Collegiate Athletic Association (NCAA). Well over 100,000 women now take part in intercollegiate sports. The figure for men is 170,000.
- The AIAW first allowed athletic scholarships in 1973. Last year some 10,000 girls from over 400 schools received such grants, worth at least $7,000,000.
- In 1972, the first all-women's mini-marathon in New York's Central Park drew 78 entries. Last May (1978), 4360 competitors entered the race.

—*Time (1978)*

Because of the tremendous interest and background many youngsters have in sports, parents and teachers can unite these students' passion for play, competition, and recognition with some sensible reading and writing experiences. In the area of sports, as perhaps seldom in youngsters' academic training, it is possible to match "the right material, with the right student, at the right time."

The genuinely strong contribution sports can make, as a basis of practice and preparation for reading and writing in all academic areas, lies in the bed of motivation and interest a majority of young people harbor for the world of athletics. These factors can often become the propellants that start and keep many students reading and writing.

The unavoidable truth, which frequently becomes obscured or buried by curriculum guides, course syllabi, assigned textbooks, and required reading lists, is that *pupils will never achieve broad reading or writing maturity and competency until they want to read and want to write!* And ultimately, interests determine whether, and to what extent, the student will read and write.

The essence of most reading and writing difficulties in school may be attributed to students' poor mental attitudes that spring from the absence of motivation or interest for a particular subject. Furthermore, this prevalent lack of interest forms the root of many youngsters' failure to acquire critical reading or writing abilities which equip them for general academic success.

> A teacher cannot force his pupils to like what he likes in reading, and if the reader has no taste for what he reads, all the time is wasted. There are no books in this world that everybody must read, but only books that a person must read at a certain time in a given place under given circumstances and at a given period of his life.
>
> —*Lin Yutang*

The above quotation (1937, p. 379) summarizes the statements above. Making sense out of reading and writing is the key to promoting life-long learning habits that lead to intellectual, emotional, and spiritual growth. Through sports, parents and teachers have a *special* "academic" vehicle with which they can not only help make reading and writing significant ventures, but use students' intense desire to improve sports knowledge and performance as the foundation of numerous meaningful literary activities.

Bibliography

Coleman, J.C. *Abnormal Psychology and Modern Life*. Glenview, IL: Scott Foresman and Co., 1964, 103.

"Here Come the Girls." *Time*, June 26, 1978.

Malcolm X, and Haley, A. *The Autobiography of Malcolm X*. New York: Ballantine Books, 1964, 179.

Yutang, L. *The Importance of Living*. New York: Capricorn Books, 1974, pp. 179, 388–89.

Sports-Related Reading and Writing Activities for Students in Elementary and Middle School Years

To read well, that is to read true books in a true spirit, is a noble exercise, and one that will task the reader more than any exercise which the customs of the day esteem. It requires a training such as the athletes underwent, the steady intention, almost of the whole life to this object.
—*Henry David Thoreau, 1817–1862*

Many people associate reading and writing with those who are more academically inclined. In effect, they see reading, writing, and sports as strange bedfellows and have difficulty understanding that those interested in sports or physical fitness can be good readers and writers too. This perspective is injurious for several reasons:

1. It confines reading and writing to school-based curricula.

2. It disassociates reading/writing and the development of critical thinking skills from sports, sports figures, and sports fans.

3. It refutes the connections in learning between mind and body; thought and action.

4. It discounts reading and writing as favorable methods:
   - to bolster the acquisition of playing or performance skills.
   - to make use of an individual's store of information, knowledge, and interest in sports as a basis for expanding learning and literacy.
   - to unfold innumerable mental and physical health concepts students of all ages can develop and apply toward happy, wholesome living.

Parents and teachers can make good use of supplemental reading and writing instructional activities that incorporate sports as an overall theme. These efforts should be made with the understanding that the listless connection that exists between many young people and reading or writing activities is not always the result of their inability to read, write, or complete assignments. More frequently it is because they are not motivated to apply themselves, fail to evolve good study/work habits or skills, and consequently are not committed to becoming effective readers and writers.

The following sports-related reading and writing activities have been developed to attract many young people who are interested in or identify with athletes and athletics. These are not meant to be complete instructional packages; rather they serve as models from which parents and teachers may devise their own. The activities guide and suggest rather than dictate ways to enhance students' reading and writing skills. They should not be employed as simply paper and pencil "drill work."

A more appropriate approach would consist of using the ideas and materials to stimulate group discussion or broader individual projects. At times, students may even be encouraged to rewrite or concoct alternative sports-based reading and writing activities that are more imaginative, comprehensive, or appealing to their personal interests. Parents and teachers can also gain valuable assistance from older students, letting them act as tutors using these activities with younger or less able youngsters. They might also act as follow-up exercises and reinforcement for performance-based instruction or serve as a means of motivating many students who would not otherwise be literate.

Elementary School
Activities

Get Equipped!
Reading Olympics

Sport: General

Purpose: To increase a student's knowledge of the function of vowels or consonants within words; to encourage creative writing.

Materials: Mail-order catalog or newspaper ads for sports equipment, scissors, glue, paper, pencil

Discussion: While consonant sounds are fairly stable in English, vowel sounds are variable. This can cause a good deal of difficulty for some students. Before a student is able to read fluently, s/he must gain mastery over both consonant and vowel sounds. Parents and teachers can take advantage of a student's familiarity with words related to sports equipment to teach these phonic elements.

Directions: Cut out pictures of athletic equipment from mail-order catalogs or from newspaper advertisements. These ads contain an assortment of commonly used words to describe the equipment. Glue pictures on a sheet of paper and number each picture. Beside each picture, write the name of the particular piece of equipment leaving blanks in the place of vowels or consonants. (Depending upon your emphasis, have the student supply vowels or consonants.) On another sheet of paper, glue the names of the equipment which have been extracted from the newspaper advertising or catalog description.

The following activities may be used:

1.   r__cq__ __tb__ll r__cq__ __t

   or

   __a__ __ue__ __a__ __   __a__ __ue__

2.   sk__ v__st

   or

   __ __i __e__ __

3

3. c_mb_ w_t_r sk_s

or

__o___o_ __a_e_ ___i_

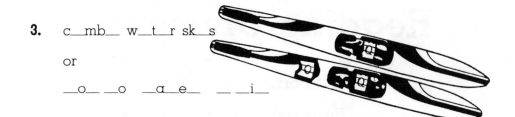

4. b_sk_tb_ll sh__

or

__a__e__a__ __ __oe

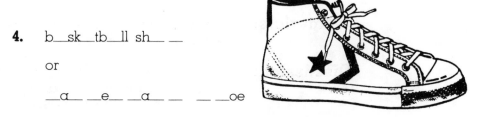

5. b_s_b_ll gl_v_

or

__a_e_a__ __ __o_e

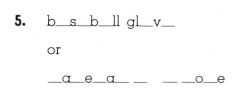

6. t_nn_s r_cq__t

or

__e__i__ __a__ue_

7. m_t_cr_ss b_c_cl_

or

__o__o__ __o__ __ __icy__e

8. s_cc_r sh__

or

__o__e__ __ __oe

9. l_g w__ __ght

or

__e_ __ei __ __ __

10. b__s__b__ll c__p

or

__a_e_a_ __ __a

11. b__sk__tb__ll

or

__a__ __e__ __a__ __

12. g__lf cl__b

or

__o__ __ __ __u__

13. t__nn__s sh__ __

or

__e__ __i__ __ __oe

14. s__cc__r b__ll

or

__o__ e__ __a__ __

Answers, page 71

Follow-Up Activity: Specify a particular phonic element such as long or short "e" or "r" controlled vowels. Ask the student to locate the specified element in the words completed in the previous activity. The student should list as many words as possible for a specified sound. A sample list has been provided below:

---

  r   controlled vowels (as the sound in the word "bird"): water, soccer

  e   short sound (as the sound in the word "pet"): racquetball, racquet, vest, basketball, tennis, leg

 au sound (as the sound of a before double l in the word "fall"): ball

  i   long sound (as the sound in the word "bind"): bicycle

 ei   long a sound (as the sound in the word "freight"): weight

  e   silent e (at the end of a word as in "have"): glove

  c   hard sound (k) (as in the word "coat"): combo, racquet, soccer

  c   soft sound (s) (frequently before e, i, or y, as in the words "celery," "city," or "cyclopse"): bicycle

  a   short sound (as in the word "bat"): cap, basketball, racquet

  a   long sound (as in the word "cape"): baseball

NOTE:

A particular word may be pronounced in several different ways depending upon the speaker's dialect, i.e., the word "tennis" may be pronounced by some to have a short "i" as the first vowel sound rather than a short "e."

Wanted! Heroes and Heroines!

Sport: General

Purpose: To develop a student's ability to do associative reasoning by asking him/her to classify several sports figures with their respective events; to classify various figurative expressions with specific sports.

Materials: Car racing track, pencil, dictionary

Discussion: Classifying information is one important reading skill required to organize ideas. Sports heroes and heroines are role models for many students. Great athletes are recognized for their abilities in specific events. Parents and teachers can use written descriptions of various sports figures to improve a youngster's ability to make associations and to develop his/her vocabulary skills as well.

Directions: Parents or teachers introduce the student to the race track puzzle. To get to the finish line, the student must first complete all the "riddles" by filling in the blanks with the name of the correct sport associated with each clue. If the child does not know the meaning of one of the underlined words in a particular riddle, help him/her locate it in the dictionary. Provide the correct pronunciations of these words and discuss various meanings for them.

RIDDLES:

1. This is Richard Petty. He is a speed merchant, meaning a very fast performer. What sport is he in?_____

2. This is Nadia Comaneci. She has great stretching form. What sport is she in?_____

3. This is Rocky Marciano. He was a great pugilist. What sport was he in?_____

4. This is Jim Brown. He was an outstanding running back in his day. What sport was he in?_____

5. Here is Maurice Richard. He could hit the puck with incredible strength. What sport was he in?_____

6. Here is Ted Williams. He had a fabulous batting average. What sport was he in? _____

7. Here is Wilt Chamberlain. He is very tall and did well dunking the ball through the hoop. What sport was he in?_____

8. Here is Pele. He began developing his skills by kicking a rag-filled sock. What sport was he in?_____

Answers, page 71

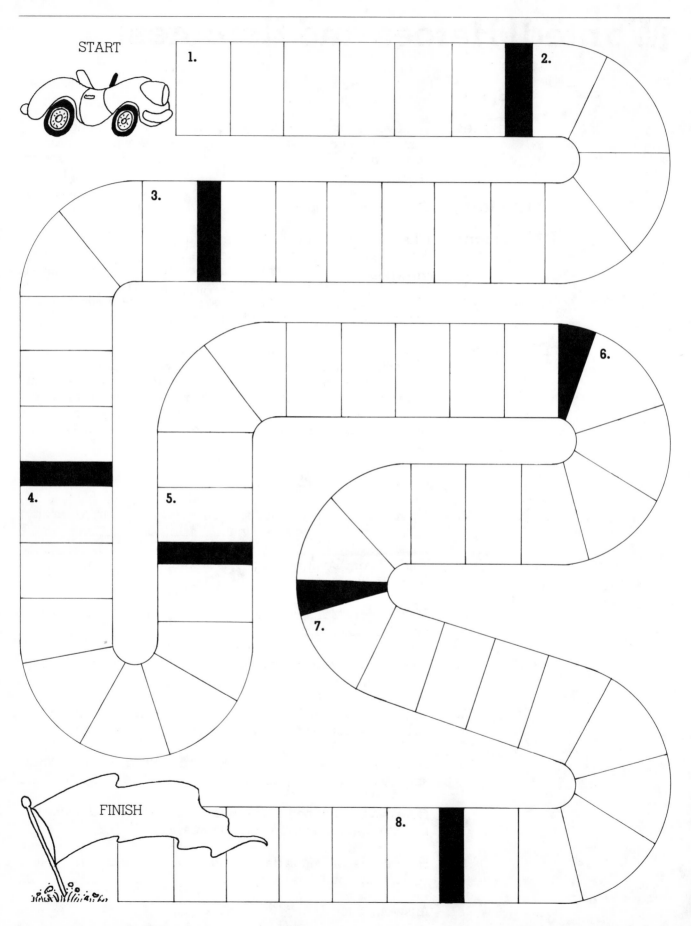

START

1.

2.

3.

4.

5.

6.

7.

8.

FINISH

Follow-Up Activity #1:
Can you make the right associations? The words below are used in the sports mentioned previously. Do you know in which sport they are used? In the following 4 columns, you will find a variety of words. See how many you can place in the right categories under the appropriate pictures on the following pages. Some of these terms may relate to more than one sport.

hoop	throw-in	center	balance
helmet	base	heading	track
forward	fumble	amplitude	heeling
key	offside	grandstand	horse
race	double play	mechanics	lap
stretch	first down	dismount	shot
tackle	kick	speed	puck
cartwheel	roundoff	vault	knockout
tires	crew	pit stop	fly ball
punch	dancing	box	fullback
kickoff	touchdown	left hook	foul
round	home plate	stick	penalty box
free throw	strike	catcher	skates
pitcher	guard	pop fly	rink
dribble	goalie	out cold	lightweight

Answers, page 71

BASKETBALL

_____
_____
_____
_____
_____
_____
_____
_____

HOCKEY

_____
_____
_____
_____
_____
_____
_____
_____
_____
_____
_____

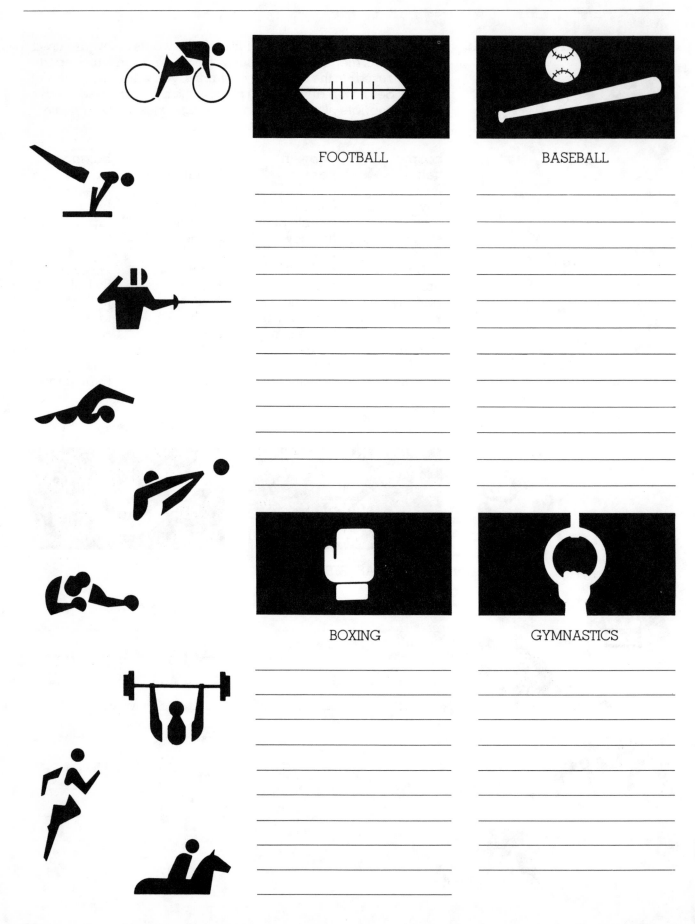

FOOTBALL

BASEBALL

BOXING

GYMNASTICS

SOCCER

STOCK CAR RACING

Follow-Up Activity #2: To reinforce the idea of heroes and heroines in sports, read the article that appears on the following page to the student. Since the writer of this sports story addresses an adult audience, it is necessary to discuss or substitute some of the vocabulary and expressions he uses before, during, and after reading the material to the student. This should provide interesting vocabulary and language enrichment activity for the student and give you the chance to discuss the significant role of the hero/heroine. Some of the words and expressions you may wish to explain or change are listed below:

State of the Union address	signature scratch	compassion
vanquished	category	plugged
triumph	those who offered life and limb	regent
sandwiched in	reassessment	revered
transfixed	researched	justice
hero stockpile	coveted award	prompted
idols		army of potentials

Felix McKnight /*The making of heroes*

President Reagan told us at the conclusion of his recent State of the Union address that we do, indeed, still have heroes who come in various forms—but all cast from a familiar mold.

He said, "Don't let anyone tell you that America's best days are behind her—that the American spirit has been vanquished. We've seen it triumph too often in our lives to stop believing in it now."

If the President could have been sandwiched in with the 1,200 at Loews Anatole hotel ballroom Wednesday night; if he could have seen the faces of the young who sat transfixed for two hours, he would have come away feeling very secure about his hero stockpile.

It was the 17th annual banquet of the All Sports Association and the subject was heroes—past, present and future. The place was loaded with live subjects. A thousand stories could have been told about them. Many were. Not a line slipped by the young who worshipped their idols and charged them with ballpoint pen for a signature scratch on their programs.

I've always reacted to identifying sports figures as "heroes"—to be lumped because of athletic achievement into the same category with those who offered life and limb to the preservation of peace and individual liberty. Or to the unknowns of science who used heroic patience and skill in discoveries directed to the well-being of mankind.

It always seemed a bit shallow to picture the guy who made the winning touchdown or whammed the World Series winning home run as a "hero." But, the faces of the young and the conduct of their idols have brought on reassessment.

Maybe the President was right. Maybe there is a definite place for their special kind of heroes.

The young, and the old, arose in acclaim as Dallas Cowboy Tony Dorsett came forward to accept the evening's highest honor—the Field Scovell Award.

Field Scovell?

A new definition of "hero" came on as Tony Dorsett beautifully accepted, noting that he had researched Field Scovell, that he now better understood what went into the making of heroes. That he would, to the best of his ability, carry with honor the coveted national award that bore the name of a man who had made it with decency, honor and compassion.

The young persons in the hall had an idol talking to them and they were listening and learning that bums don't make it to hero.

They heard that Field Scovell was an old North Dallas High-Texas Aggie athlete who once was a kid who worshipped his idols. He did well as athlete, even better as citizen.

He plugged, became successful, served on the Dallas Independent School District Board of Trustees, the Dallas Parks Board and as a regent at Texas Tech University where his son and daughter were high honor graduates—the son captain and quarterback of the football team.

They heard that Field Scovell was revered and known around the nation—not just as chairman of the Cotton Bowl Athletic Association, but as a man who knows reason, the rules of the game, fairness and justice.

They heard of his work with youth, his community, his concern for his fellow man. All the qualities that prompted the All Sports Association, in 1965, to establish the Field Scovell Award that has been won by Frank Broyles, Sandy Koufax, Arthur Ashe, Darrell Royal, the 1970 Cowboys, Bob Lilly, Jack Nicklaus, Fran Tarkenton, Ferguson Jenkins, Roger Staubach, Forrest Gregg, Tom Landry, Earl Campbell, Bear Bryant, Randy White and Tony Dorsett.

Mr. President, don't worry about future heroes. Those who heard the Field Scovell story, and millions of others like them, are your army of potentials.

Dallas Times Herald (Sep. 17, 1981)

Once Upon a Sport

Sport: General

Purpose: To develop a student's creative writing skills; to strengthen word recognition.

Materials: Paper, pencil, list of story starters

Discussion: Parents and teachers can use the topic of sports to interest students in creative writing. Many students have problems generating ideas when they are asked to write a story. A good technique is to provide the students with story starters for which they write endings. Sports-related story starters will motivate interested students to write. These stories will also serve as good vehicles to practice word-recognition skills and to pinpoint difficulties a student might be having in this area. These could include problems recognizing basic sight word vocabulary or identifying the beginnings, middles, and endings of words.

Directions: Provide the student with the beginning to a sports-related story. Have him/her complete the story and draw a picture to illustrate it. Then have the student read the story and discuss the illustration.

STORY STARTERS:

1. Joey and Tom were playing baseball in an empty lot next door to the Browns'. Joey hit a fly ball straight through an upstairs window of the Browns' home. The 2 boys were scared, but they knew the Browns would be on vacation for another week—Finish the story.

2. Sue was in her first 600 meter bicycle race. She was pedaling comfortably in third place after the first half of the race. What she and the other bicyclers did not know was that a cruel prankster had spilled grease 50 meters from the finish line—Finish the story.

3. The annual football game between the cross-town high school rivals was tied. One of the officials blew his whistle and made a questionable call. An angry fan grabbed a nearby bottle—Finish the story.

4. The 2 boxers were well into the ninth round when a fan seated high up in the arena let out a blood-curdling scream—Finish the story.

5. It was 15 minutes before the start of the big game. The coach was giving his team last-minute instructions when he noticed a strange-looking man standing at the door of the locker room listening to every word being said—Finish the story.

6. The horses came out of the gate like a shot. As they passed the one-half mile post, the jockey riding the lead horse felt his mount's rear leg give a sudden twist. He knew this great runner must be in terrible pain, but they were winning—Finish the story.

7. Ted and his friend were shopping near the toy store one day when a brand new soccer ball rolled out the door. There appeared to be nobody around—Finish the story.

8. The young boy was the first-string quarterback on his neighborhood football team. He sometimes thought to himself that it was only because his father was the head coach—Finish the story.

9. As the boy rounded third base headed for home, he thought about the time he—Finish the story.

10. Anne was skating down her street with the new skates she received for her birthday when—Finish the story.

11. The 2 boys were jogging through their neighborhood one morning when a strange-looking van drove by—Finish the story.

12. Steve was fishing in a nearby lake when he hooked a—Finish the story.

13. Bob was on his first solo deer hunting trip. He saw, what looked at a distance to be a buck, but as he crept closer, he noticed it was a young deer which had probably strayed from its mother—Finish the story.

14. The big go-cart race was scheduled for Saturday. Rumors of sabotage were circulating through the neighborhood—Finish the story.

15. It was the beginning of the championship game of the Stanley Cup playoffs when a fan threw something on the ice—Finish the story.

Follow-Up Activity: To strengthen word-recognition skills, have the student circle each word in his/her story that contains the suffixes "ed," "es," "s," or "ing." S/he should list the circled words from his/her story as in the example below. Then discuss with the student the root word and how the suffix alters its meaning.

WORD	SUFFIX	ROOT
touching	touch	ing
skated	skate	ed
runs	run	s
bats	bat	s
calls	call	s

Seek and You Shall Find

Sport: General

Purpose: To develop a student's spelling skills and to increase his/her vocabulary.

Materials: Pencils, paper

Discussion: Many students, for many reasons, are reluctant readers. As a result, it is not uncommon for them to be poor spellers and to have limited reading vocabularies. However, because sports are interesting for many of these students, parents or teachers can take advantage of this situation and introduce sports-related reading and writing activities. Often, while these students will balk at typical literary activities, they will approach these enthusiastically.

Directions: Have the student examine the following clues and provide the name of the sport described in the adjacent blank. Provide assistance if s/he has difficulty spelling an answer.

CLUES:

1. This sport is a very rough game in which leather balls are used. This game is similar to football. _____

2. This sport is a game in which you try to knock down 10 pins.

   _____

3. This sport is a fast-moving game which is played on ice.

   _____

4. This sport is a game played on a court. A small ball is hit back and forth with a racket. _____

5. This sport is a game in which a raised net is used to separate both teams. _____

6. This sport is a contest in which a "knockout" can occur.

   _____

7. This sport takes place in the water. _____

8. This sport involves putting a small white ball in a hole.

   _____

9. In this sport, the ball is kicked or bounced off the head.

   _____

10. In this sport, the ball is pitched and hit. _____

11. In this sport, a touchdown or field goal is scored. _____

12. In this sport, the fastest runners or highest jumpers win.

_____

13. This sport involves trying to catch the biggest one.

_____

14. In this sport, a round ball is dribbled and put into the hoop.

_____

15. In this sport, you try to pin your opponent. _____

Answers, page 72

Follow-Up Activity: Find the names of the 15 sports listed below which are hidden in the puzzle. These names may be written across, down, diagonally, or backwards.

y	b	g	u	r	f	s	d	q	l	d	c	l	t
o	f	p	n	l	d	i	c	m	l	b	l	a	r
c	d	e	x	l	o	m	b	f	a	a	r	w	j
g	i	t	r	a	c	k	s	o	b	x	n	p	q
n	o	v	s	b	b	d	f	t	t	o	m	h
i	b	o	g	e	s	b	o	l	e	i	g	t	o
h	f	l	n	s	h	o	l	n	k	b	n	v	c
s	u	l	i	a	f	a	n	r	s	d	i	w	k
i	b	e	x	b	b	i	o	p	a	z	l	k	e
f	d	y	o	p	s	o	d	c	b	p	t	m	y
b	s	b	b	g	n	i	m	m	i	w	s	z	r
a	t	a	z	h	o	d	s	o	c	c	e	r	a
c	m	l	b	o	w	l	i	n	g	l	r	s	d
e	n	l	r	t	c	h	f	t	n	a	w	m	p

Answers, page 72

Sports Analogies

Sport: General

Level: Elementary-Middle School

Purpose: To develop a student's comprehension through analogies.

Materials: Pencil, paper, list of sports-related analogies

Discussion: Analogies are useful in expanding comprehension skills because they explore relationships between words and serve to transfer those relationships to new groups of words. For example, to solve the following analogy:

a hit is to baseball as a first down is to _____

one must first determine what the relationship is between a hit in baseball and a first down in football. Once the student sees the relationship, s/he can use his/her knowledge of football to make a similar association.

Directions: Discuss the concept of analogies with the student using the above example. Then ask him/her to match each statement on the left to its analogous partner on the right. If the student has difficulty, help explain the association that each pair of statements contains. Below is an example:

_12_	A. umpire is to baseball as	1. club is to golf
_____	B. touchdown is to football as	2. error is to baseball
_____	C. racquet is to tennis as	3. manager is to baseball
_____	D. quarterback is to pass as	4. Indianapolis is to auto racing
_____	E. end zone is to touchdown as	5. bull's-eye is to archery
_____	F. coach is to football as	6. extra inning is to baseball
_____	G. turnover is to basketball as	7. pitcher is to pitch
_____	H. Super Bowl is to football as	8. NBA is to basketball
_____	I. Wimbledon is to tennis	9. goal is to soccer
_____	J. overtime is to basketball as	10. World Series is to baseball
_____	K. hole is to golf as	11. home plate is to run
_____	L. NASL is to soccer as	12. referee is to football

Answers, page 72

Follow-Up Activity: SPORTSENTRATION

Write half of each statement below on a separate 3″ × 5″ index card. Mix the cards and lay them face down. Ask the student (2 may play) to turn over 2 cards and try to match a pair. When s/he makes a match, s/he keeps the cards and turns over 2 more. This continues until the student fails to make a match. It then becomes the other student's turn. The game is over when all of the cards are matched. The winner is the student with the most matching pairs. When the game is complete, have the student explain the relationship in each of the analogies.

Roper is to calf	as	Tackler is to ball carrier

SUGGESTED STATEMENTS:

1. Wimbledon is to tennis as the British Open is to golf.

2. Diamond is to baseball as gridiron is to football.

3. Pigskin is to football as horsehide is to baseball.

4. Quarter is to basketball as inning is to baseball.

5. Decathalon is to men's track as pentathalon is to women's track.

6. Eleven is to football as 5 is to basketball.

7. Pitcher is to catcher as passer is to receiver.

8. Thirty seconds is to football as 24 seconds is to basketball.

9. Ski pole is to skiing as oar is to rowing.

10. Gymnast is to trampoline as diver is to diving board.

11. Gymnasium is to basketball as swimming pool is to swimmer.

12. Base is to baseball as yard line is to football.

Titles Away!

Sport: General

Purpose: To develop a student's ability to make inferences by introducing several brief sports stories which s/he must read and entitle.

Materials: Pencil

Discussion: Parents and teachers can use "sports sketches" to teach a student to make inferences and do some creative thinking. It is important that students learn to "read between the lines." School work necessitates reading beyond a literal or factual level and frequently requires students to make interpretations of what they have read. This activity aids in this cause.

Directions: Read each story below. Then have the student write a title that best fits the story. See the example given:

On the Ball

Someday William Walter, age 11, would like to be a pro baseball player. He has a good start.

William is a ballboy for the Texas Rangers. He got the job when he was only 7 years old because he was a loyal fan.

William is on the job at all home games during the season. He retrieves foul balls hit to right field.

Before games, he runs errands and chases balls at batting practice. Between innings, he often warms up the visiting team's right fielders.

William is paid $7 per game. He is saving the money to go to college.

The National Junior Olympic Multisport Championships will be held June 21–24th. Other Junior Olympic championships such as weightlifting, wrestling, basketball, and swimming are held at other times and places.

There are 7 sports in the Multisport Championships. These are: track and field, gymnastics, judo, trampoline and tumbling, synchronized swimming, diving, and wrestling. All athletes have to qualify to compete. These athletes are excited to be competing in Dallas, Texas. Many of them are a long way from home.

Houston, Texas, December 27, 1981, was the scene for the Punt, Pass, and Kick contest. Thousands of fans watched from the stands. Millions watched on television.

Six football champs, ages 8–13, went out on the field and picked up their trophies. They had punted, passed, and kicked their way to the top. They had been in 6 contests and won at each level from local to national.

"I was calm," Wayne Mayo said to the *Houston Daily News*.

"I was beside myself," Aaron Mitchell told the reporter.

The 1981 winners will be announced at the Super Bowl on January 24, 1982, in Pontiac, Michigan.

Most 18-year-old boys like to drive fast cars, date, play ball, and listen to rock music. However, Lawrence Price is usually too busy horsing around to become involved in those things. He is a professional jockey and the newest superstar of horse racing. The superboy is 5'2" tall and weighs 95 pounds.

Lawrence is an only child and grew up in Kentucky. Both of his parents train thoroughbreds.

From his earnings as a jockey, Lawrence bought a sky-blue Trans Am. But he enjoys life most when he is in the saddle, riding a race horse to the finish line.

Arthur Adams is a giant who plays forward on the basketball court. In 8 seasons with the Dallas Mavericks, Arthur has been selected to play in 6 NBA All-Star games.

He is 6'10" tall. He is an excellent shooter and a strong defensive player.

Before joining the Dallas Mavericks, Arthur was a star player for the University of Houston Cougars. In one game, he scored 45 points to become Houston's all-time leading scorer. In his senior year he led the Cougars to their first NCAA Championship.

The Dallas Mavericks basketball team began shining a lot brighter the day they signed Arthur Adams. He is a true star!

Ralph Smallwood is a pro golf player. He has won the British Open, the Masters, the Tucson Open, and the Bob Hope Desert Classic. Last year alone, he won more than $210,000.

He is currently the leading money winner on the circuit. Last week he had a record setting 12 under par in the Tournament of Champions. During the second round of the tournament, he had 10 consecutive birdies.

Smallwood is considered the top pro golfer in the world. He is recognized as one of the best drivers and the most accurate putter in the PGA.

Answers, page 72

Follow-Up Activity: Construct sentences underlining those terms with which the student may be unfamiliar. Under each sentence, list 3 terms, one of which is inferentially related to the underlined word in each sentence. Have the student circle the correct word in each instance. Discuss his/her answers.

1. William began to <u>warm up</u> before the game to get ready.

   exercise   sing   do homework

2. Betty and Carla performed together like ballet dancers as they did the <u>synchronized</u> swimming to music.

   rock and roll   moved as one   forced

3. <u>Judo</u> is a sport that teaches a person self-defense.

   religion   movie   a system of exercise

4. The <u>thoroughbred</u> neighed as he came down the home stretch.

   dog   cow   horse

5. The star <u>forward</u> on the basketball team was rebounding all night.

   the player by the basket   the player by the free-throw line

   the player sitting on the bench

6. The golfer shot a <u>birdie</u> to win the hole.

   bird   a score on a hole of one under par   a golf club

7. The pro golfer used a <u>driver</u> on the par 3 hole.

   chauffeur   a type of golf club—No. 1 wood   rope

8. Once the golfer was on the green, he used the <u>putter</u> to roll the ball on the ground and into the hole.

   racket   stick   golf club

   Answers, page 73

Amazing Words from Baseball

Sport: Baseball

Purpose: To develop a student's reading, writing, and spelling abilities.

Materials: Prepared maze, pencil, a list of words from baseball

Discussion: Through the use of baseball terminology, a student can enjoy learning to read, write, and spell. Numerous baseball terms are put into a maze to test the student's reading, writing, and spelling ability.

Directions: Present the following maze to a student, inserting words that are associated with baseball. Tell him/her to begin with the baseball player and end at the baseball by going through the lanes that contain words from the game of baseball that are spelled correctly. If the student selects a path containing an incorrectly spelled word, it will lead to a dead end. S/he must follow the words that are spelled accurately in order to get to the baseball and exit the maze.

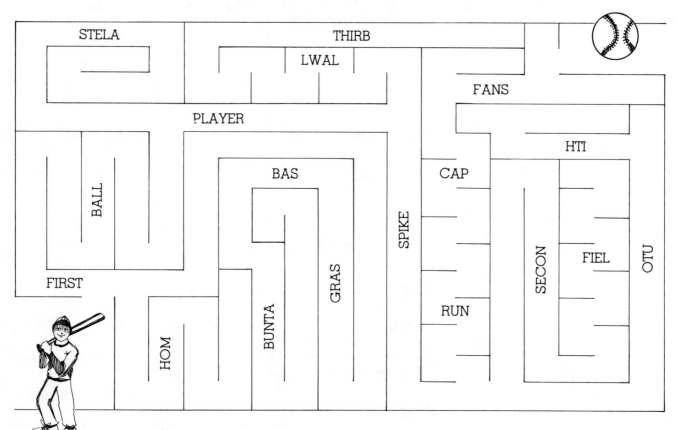

Answer, page 73

Follow-Up Activity: Discuss these words with the student. Ask him/her to write each one and check for accurate spelling. Then tell the student to make up sentences using these words.

Getting It Together—Baseball Compounds

Sport: Baseball

Purpose: To increase a student's recognition and understanding of compound words.

Materials: Lightweight, light-colored tagboard; black marker; brightly-colored yarn (8 different colors); crayons (same colors as yarn); metal brads; hole punch

Discussion: Recognition of the components of compound words is a structural-analysis skill which can help a student identify those words when s/he encounters them in print. Baseball uses a large number of compounds in its terminology. This activity can lend variety and interest to the teaching of these terms (example: horsehide) by exposing the student to a variety of combined word forms. This is an individual activity which is self-correcting.

Directions: On the left side of the tagboard, list the first part of the compounds below using a black marker:

baseball	playoff	infield	shortstop
batboy	fastball	outfield	strikeout

Immediately to the right of each word part, insert a brad and tie the end of a length of yarn around it—use a different colored yarn for each word. Leave the yarn dangling and make sure it is long enough to reach to the other side.

On the right side of the cardboard, list the second parts of the compounds in scrambled order. Immediately in front of each of these words, punch a small hole large enough for the insertion of the yarn.

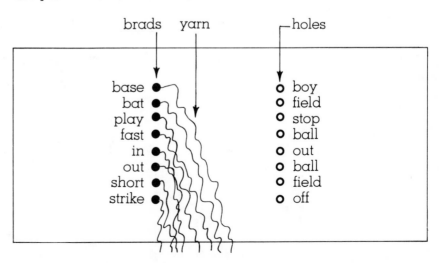

On the back of the tagboard, color a square beside each hole which corresponds to the color of yarn that should come through the hole.

Show the student the card and tell him/her that compound words are 2 words that fit together and become a single word. The cards contain compound words that come from baseball terminology and can be divided into their separate parts. The first part of each compound is on the left. Tell the student to put the yarn by each beginning word part through the hole beside the word that completes the compound (example: base and ball go together to make baseball). When s/he is finished, the card can be turned over and checked by the student. The colored squares on the back tell which color of yarn should go through the holes. If the student has made any errors, correct them. Then the student can read the compound words that s/he has just put together.

Follow-Up Activity: Fill in the blanks using these compound words. Each word may be used only once.

baseball	playoff	infield	shortstop
batboy	fastball	outfield	strikeout

1. The _____ helps the team by chasing balls and carrying bats.

2. When the Tigers beat the Yankees on the last day of the season, a _____ was necessary to decide the champion.

3. The first baseman plays in the _____.

4. The _____ plays between second and third base.

5. Our _____ team won the championship.

6. The third out was a _____.

7. The centerfielder caught the ball in the _____.

8. Nolan Ryan is a pitcher known for his _____.

Answers, page 73

Seek and Find: Baseball Words

Sport: Baseball

Purpose: To develop a student's reading, writing, and spelling ability.

Materials: "Seek and Find" puzzle, pencil, words from baseball

Discussion: By using terms from baseball, a student can enjoy learning to read, write, and spell. Many words can be put into a "Seek and Find" puzzle to test the student's reading, writing, and spelling ability.

Directions: Present the following puzzle. Tell the student that there are many words from baseball hidden in the puzzle, and s/he should read and follow these directions.

In the puzzle below, you will find many hidden baseball words. Locate as many of the following words as you can and circle them. The words may appear left to right, right to left, straight up and down, or diagonally:

bat	field
baseball	bunt
base	steal
helmet	run
player	walk
fans	fly

o	p	l	a	y	e	r	h	f	w	x	z	w
o	g	f	e	d	f	d	e	n	i	y	b	a
b	a	s	e	b	a	l	l	v	c	e	c	l
a	h	i	j	a	n	p	m	g	j	k	l	k
t	r	u	n	s	s	g	e	b	u	n	t	d
a	y	l	f	e	u	r	t	s	t	e	a	l

Answers, page 73

Follow-Up Activity: Have the student spell the words out loud. Ask him/her to make up sentences using these words and write them in the spaces provided. Then ask the student to check for spelling accuracy.

Sight Word Baseball

Sport: Baseball

Purpose: To reinforce and review sight vocabulary—those words recognized as wholes and requiring no phonetic analysis.

Materials: Construction paper, scissors, glue, black marker, list of high-frequency sight words, paper, pencil

Discussion: The recognition of certain words that appear consistently throughout printed material is absolutely essential to fluent reading, especially in the beginning stages. These words are taught and learned most easily as sight words. Many of them are not particularly meaningful in and of themselves and are therefore not very interesting or recognizable to some students. In addition, since the teaching of words for instant sight recognition necessitates repetition, students often become bored with the drills required to learn these words. This activity is a means for reviewing sight words in a sports context that is interesting to many students and yet provides the necessary practice.

The student must read and pronounce each word, then use it in a sentence so s/he recognizes its function and purpose. The student then provides a definition for the word in his/her own words, which places additional emphasis on word meaning. Finally, s/he writes the word to reinforce learning it.

Directions: Construct a baseball diamond similar to the following illustration. Cut the infield out of green construction paper and glue it onto a piece of white construction paper. Use a black marker to draw the bases and baselines.

Cut out circles approximately 2" in diameter, decorate with baseball stitching, and write a sight word on each with the black marker.

Use sight words of high frequency such as the following:

a, above, across, after, again, air, all, am, and, are, ask, back, be, before, black, book, boy, came, can, children, could, day, did, didn't, down, end, feet, find, five, four, get, girl, go, good, had, hand, help, here, home, I, is, it, just, like, little, look, make, man, me, my, name, new, now, old, open, out, play, really, right, run, said, school, she, six, some, table, that, the, then, there, they, think, three, today, two, under, very, want, was, we, went, what, where, which, who, why, work, year, you

Once the materials are constructed, set the baseball diamond in front of the student and give him/her a sheet of paper and a pencil. Establish the purpose for the game by telling the student to practice reading some words that need to be recognized very quickly because they are used repeatedly in the materials we all read. Then give the following directions:

1. When I put the baseball with a word on it on home plate, say the word. If you recognize and pronounce the word accurately, this moves the ball to first base. (Give him/her 3 chances, or "strikes" and if s/he doesn't get it correct, pronounce the word and reintroduce it later.)

2. When the ball is on first base, you can move it to second by using it in a sentence—jot these down for use later.

3. When the ball is on second base, you can move it to third by defining it or telling what it means in your own words.

4. When the ball is on third base, you can get it home and earn a run by writing it correctly on your paper.

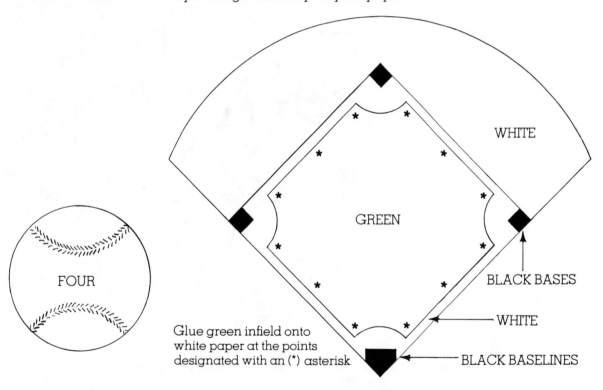

FOUR

Glue green infield onto white paper at the points designated with an (*) asterisk

Follow-Up Activity: For review and reinforcement purposes, copy onto paper bats, the sentences that the student generates with the sight words. These can be fashioned from colored construction paper. Ask the student to read each sentence aloud and let him/her keep the bat if s/he reads the sentence correctly.

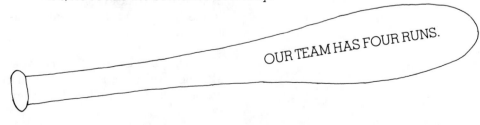

OUR TEAM HAS FOUR RUNS.

Speaking of Baseball

Sport: Baseball

Purpose: To develop a student's ability to read stories, identify quotations, and designate the speaker in dialog by recognizing various signal words.

Materials: Pencil

Discussion: Parents and teachers can use a story related to baseball to teach a student to recognize quotations and identify signal words that indicate a particular character's statements.

WHO IS TALKING?

We can both pitch! All we have to do is rotate.

You're crazy! It is impossible.

Directions: Tell the student that often a writer uses quotation marks and signal words to tell a reader who is doing the talking in a story. A good reader must learn to recognize quotation marks and signal words to follow the story line.

The players above are giving us their different ideas about pitching in a game of baseball. In a story without pictures, the reader must rely on quotation marks and signal words like "said," "asked," and "told" to identify the character who is doing the talking.

Following is a baseball story. The characters are Mac and Charlie. Tell the student to read it to him/herself and underline the statements made by the 2 players.

"Hey, Charlie! Give this guy one of your curveballs. Make the ball walk and talk as it comes over the plate," said Mac.

"Well, Mac, I don't think this guy is ready for that. You better offer him something to clean his glasses," answered Charlie.

"It won't do any good for him to clean his glasses. He will think he was dreaming when the ump calls him out. Man, you have him going your way. Strike him out!" responded Mac.

Charlie wound up and let the pitch go. It was a strike.

"It was all right, Charlie! That was strike one. You just need 2 more," yelled Mac.

Charlie sent another pitch straight across the plate.

"Great! Charlie, just one more," hollered Mac.

"Mac, clean off the plate so I can throw a real curve. This is going to be an easy out!" yelled Charlie.

Charlie threw but it was not a strike. The ball sailed by just inches from the batter's eyes. Even the fans knew before the ump made the call that it was a ball.

"Charlie, settle down! You only need one good spin and you have him," counseled Mac.

"Okay, Mac. Here goes!" exclaimed Charlie.

The ball flew across the plate. However, the batter hit a foul ball. He started cursing.

Charlie knew he had the batter now. He wound up for the last time. It was a perfect pitch! The batter swung with all his might and missed. He left the plate wishing he'd never seen a baseball.

Of course Charlie left the mound in a state of joy. He had helped his team win the state championship.

"You should feel real proud, Charlie," cried Mac.

Answers, page 73

Follow-Up Activity #1:

In the following exercise, write an M beside the sentences spoken by Mac, and write C beside the sentences spoken by Charlie. An example is given.

> *C* "Okay, Mac. Here goes!"

1. ＿＿ "Great! Charlie, just one more. . . ."
2. ＿＿ "Give this guy one of your curveballs."
3. ＿＿ "Mac, clean off the plate so I can throw a real curve."
4. ＿＿ "It won't do any good for him to clean his glasses."
5. ＿＿ "Charlie, settle down!"
6. ＿＿ "It was all right, Charlie!"
7. ＿＿ "Make the ball walk and talk as it comes over the plate. . . ."
8. ＿＿ "Well, Mac, I don't think this guy is ready for that."
9. ＿＿ "That was strike one. You just need 2 more. . . ."
10. ＿＿ "You should feel real proud, Charlie. . . ."

Answers, page 74

Follow-Up Activity #2: Provide the following *cloze* activity—a procedure that consists of a written passage containing regularly spaced blanks. Direct the student to fill in each of these blanks with one of the words in the following list. Score a "grand slam" for each answer that is exactly the same as in the original story. Afterwards, let the student read the story out loud to you.

yelled   answered   cried
responded commented exclaimed
said   hollered   counseled

1. "Hey, Charlie! Give this guy one of your curveballs. Make the ball walk and talk as it comes over the plate," _____ Mac.

2. "Well, Mac, I don't think this guy is ready for that. You better offer him something to clean his glasses," _____ Charlie.

3. "It won't do any good for him to clean his glasses. He will think he was dreaming when the ump calls him out. Man, you have him going your way. Strike him out!" _____ Mac.

4. "It was all right, Charlie! That was strike one. You just need 2 more," _____ Mac.

5. "Great! Charlie, just one more," _____ Mac.

6. "Mac, clean off the plate so I can throw a real curve. This is going to be an easy out!" _____ Charlie.

7. "Charlie, settle down! You only need one good spin and you have him, _____ Mac.

8. "Okay, Mac. Here goes!" _____ Charlie.

9. "You should feel real proud, Charlie," _____ Mac.

Answers, page 74

A Sports Zoo

Sport: Baseball

Purpose: To expand a student's use of figurative language (colorful expressions) by introducing certain phrases frequently used in baseball that contain graphic references to animals.

Materials: Paper, pencils

Discussion: Frequently, we use the names of animals and phrases describing animal behavior when making reference to other human beings. Moreover, these terms are used to describe athletes and their performances. Students can learn to apply these correctly for purposes of strengthening their oral and written statements. Below are examples:

He is as wild as a <u>bronco.</u>	He is quick as a <u>cat.</u>
She moves like a <u>swan.</u>	He's sly as a <u>fox.</u>
She's as quiet as a <u>mouse.</u>	She's busy as a <u>beaver.</u>
She <u>fawns</u> all over her little brother.	He is a <u>lion</u> of a man.

Directions: Make use of figurative language by asking the student to write his/her interpretation of several representative words and expressions. Present the following list of sentences to the student which contain words or phrases from baseball using animals as references for various human behaviors. Notice the underlined words or phrases in these statements. After reading each sentence, write the meaning of the underlined word or phrase in the spaces provided.

1. Fergie Jenkins cast an <u>eagle-eyed glance</u> at the runner on first.

   _____

   _____

2. The Rangers' pitching staff felt <u>cocky</u> after 3 wins in a row knowing the next 3 games were home games. _____

   _____

   _____

3. Reggie Jackson is a winner, but some managers have accused him of being a <u>snake in the grass.</u> _____

   _____

   _____

   _____

4. First baseman Pete Rose hustles so much during a game that he is <u>dog-tired</u> when it's over. _____

_____

_____

5. That was quite a play the second baseman made when he <u>out-foxed</u> the runner. _____

_____

_____

6. The third baseman is making <u>catcalls</u> at the umpire! _____

_____

_____

7. A warning to the <u>bullheaded</u> left fielder resulted in him walking off the field. _____

_____

_____

8. Coach Foster was about to give up on his outfield because now even the center fielder was <u>horsing around!</u> _____

_____

_____

9. Playing the right field position was perfect for John since he was <u>hogging</u> all the fly balls anyway. _____

_____

_____

10. Even the team manager had something to say about our getting <u>skunked</u> in the game with Detroit. _____

_____

_____

Answers, page 74

Follow-Up Activity: The following word list contains the animal names of 10 teams, 4 from baseball and 6 from football. After reading each team's name from the word list, ask the student to match it with the corresponding sport and city in the second column by writing the correct number in the blank space.

WORD LIST: SPORT AND CITY:

_____ A. Lions   1. football; Denver
_____ B. Seahawks   2. football; Los Angeles
_____ C. Blue Jays   3. baseball; Baltimore
_____ D. Eagles   4. baseball; Chicago
_____ E. Broncos   5. baseball; Detroit
_____ F. Orioles   6. football; Seattle
_____ G. Dolphins   7. baseball; Toronto
_____ H. Cubs   8. football; Detroit
_____ I. Tigers   9. football; Philadelphia
_____ J. Rams   10. football; Miami

Answers, page 74

Free Throw

Sport: Basketball

Purpose: To develop a student's sight vocabulary by introducing him/her to homographs—words which are spelled alike but have different meanings and sometimes different pronunciations; to teach the student to use context clues in order to understand the precise meaning of a word.

Materials: Pencil, paper, sports-related newspaper or magazine article, dictionary

Discussion: The English language is composed of a rich variety of words. Unabridged dictionaries list over one-half million words while localisms, slang, and some occupational terms add thousands more to the lexicon. Parents and teachers can make good use of sports-related newspaper or magazine articles to teach a student that many words in our language may be spelled alike, yet have different pronunciations and different meanings. Frequently, it is necessary to understand the context in which a word is being used if a student wants to accurately measure an author's meaning. Below are examples:

As a coach, he is not <u>free</u> with his compliments.
"Hurry, we have to <u>free</u> his arm from the broken tree limb."
The lady said she would give me the ring <u>free</u> of charge.

"<u>Throw</u> me the ball," I yelled to the center.
The girl looked pale when she said, "I think I'm going to <u>throw</u> up!"
I told the gentleman to go ahead and <u>throw</u> away the minutes of that meeting.

Understanding homographs that appear throughout written material is important because students must make accurate interpretations if they are to discuss an author's ideas intelligently.

John Stuart Mill, in his Inaugural Address as Rector, University of St. Andrew (February 1, 1867), said:

> To question all things; never to turn away from any difficulty; to accept no doctrine either from ourselves or from other people without a rigid scrutiny by negative criticism; letting no fallacy, or incoherence, or confusion of thought, step by unperceived; above all, to insist upon having the meaning of a word clearly understood before using it, and the meaning of a pronunciation before assenting to it; these are the lessons we learn from ancient dialecticians.

Directions: Using the newspaper article on this page, ask the student to look over the title and each of the 3 columns for the purpose of underlining any words that may have multiple meanings. Allow approximately 5 minutes for this preview. Assistance may be given to those students who fail to identify a minimum of 5 words. Discuss some of these terms with the student and then ask him/her to read the full article silently. Afterwards, point out the sentences dealing with multiple-meaning words and ask the student what each means based upon how it is used in the sentence. Focus the discussion on context clues (an aid used in recognizing words whereby the surrounding word or sentences assist a reader's pronunciation or understanding of the word or words in question). Then ask the student to complete the exercises on the following pages. Below is a list of some of the homographs used in the article:

protest	offense
center	contest
combine	court
game	record
points	shots
defense	

Americans defeat Soviets in double-OT

By GIL LeBRETON
Star-Telegram Writer

BUCHAREST, Romania—A wild U.S.-Soviet semifinal in the World University Games basketball tournament overshadowed record-setting gold medal performances at the track and swimming pool Saturday as the flashy Americans downed the Soviets, 113-107, in double-overtime.

A mostly Romanian crowd of about 1,600 turned the tiny Giulesti gymnasium into a hotbox, cheering the moves of Villanova's John Pinone and LSU's Howard Carter as well as some hotly contested officials' calls that went against the Soviets.

But empty seats were abundant at the 70,000-capacity track stadium, while spectators tried to squeeze past security guards into the gym where Americans and Soviets clashed on the basketball court.

Carter scored 28 points, most of them from the outside, and Pinone collected 27, many against 7-foot-4 Soviet center Vladimir Tkachenko under the basket.

John Bagley of Boston College, Kevin Boyle of Iowa and Kevin Magee of California-Irvine worked an acrobatic inside offense against the big Soviets, and combined with North Carolina State's Sid Lowe to shake up the Soviets on defense.

"Our quickness bothers some people," said Coach Tom Davis of Boston College.

Soviet coach Vladimir Kolos and several Soviet players bitterly protested the officials' decisions that kept the Americans in the game.

With the score tied at 101 in the first overtime, a foul was called against the United States in a rebound battle under the Soviet basket. Officials at first signaled that the Soviets would get two free throws, but changed the decision seconds later, saying time had run out.

"Today the shots fell for us and didn't fall for them," said Davis.

Sergei Iovasa was the game's high scorer with 29 points for the Soviets.

Canada, which had handed the United States an 78-76 defeat the night before, beat Mexico, 81-67, and was undefeated going into its last semifinal round game against the Soviets Sunday.

Fort Worth Star Telegram (July 26, 1981)
Answers, page 75

Have the student write original sentences using the following words in the way they are used in the article. See the example given.

> <u>shots</u> The forward simply wasn't making enough shots count to win the game.

1. protest_____

    _____

2. center_____

    _____

3. combine_____

    _____

4. game_____

    _____

5. points_____

    _____

6. defense_____

    _____

7. offense_____

    _____

8. contest_____

    _____

9. court_____

    _____

10. record_____

    _____

Answers, page 75

Follow-Up Activity: Have the student work the following basketball-related puzzle. When the student has solved the 8 clues, have him/her list the letters in the vertical column to find the mystery word. The mystery word is an important part of every basketball game.

CLUES:

1. Place where a team likes to play the most.

2. The people who cheer for a team.

3. What players toss around.

4. Number of players on a basketball team.

5. Number of points a team scores for each basket.

6. A part of the game (ending punctuation of a sentence).

7. Sometimes the players do this to reach the basket.

8. A person who keeps order in a game.

Mystery Word _____ _____ _____ _____ _____ _____ _____ _____

Answers, page 75

Mix and Match

Sport: Basketball and Track

Purpose: To develop a student's fluent word-recognition skills through basketball and track terms.

Materials: Word-picture slide, clothes patterns, pencil

Discussion: The development of fluent word-recognition skills using basketball and track terms is the basis of this activity. A word-picture slide can be used to motivate students in this effort.

Directions: Present the student with a piece of posterboard with 4 slits in it.

Also present a word strip and a picture strip to slide through the slits.

Ask the student to match the picture with the word as you slide the strips into each card.

POSTERBOARD

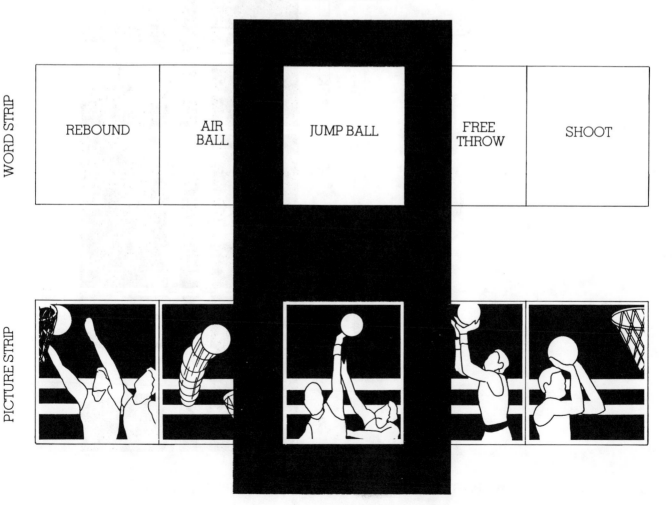

WORD STRIP

REBOUND   AIR BALL   JUMP BALL   FREE THROW   SHOOT

PICTURE STRIP

Mix and Match

WORD STRIP

| SHOOT | FREE THROW | JUMP BALL | AIR BALL | REBOUND |

BASKETBALL TERMS

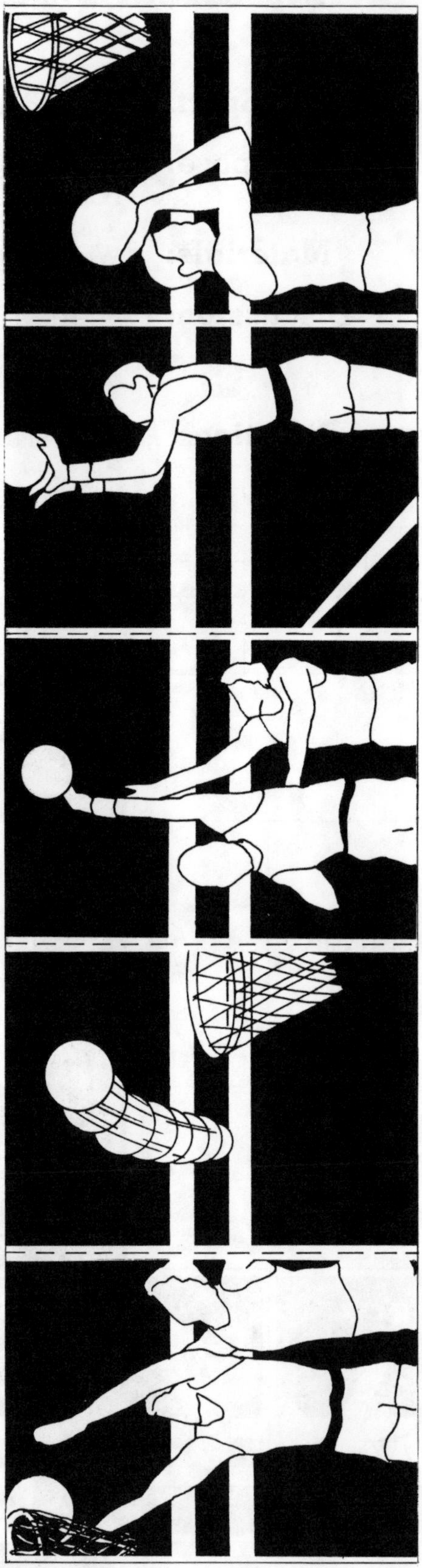

PICTURE STRIP

POLE VAULT	JAVELIN	RELAY	BROAD JUMP	HURDLES

TRACK TERMS

WORD STRIP

PICTURE STRIP

VARIATION:

Words do not have to be sequenced in the same order as the pictures.

BASKETBALL TERMS:

air ball	rim	lane	upset
air dribble	out-of-bounds	assist	half-court
free throw	screen	post	key
jump ball	pick	layup	pass
throw-in	carom	form	jump
rebound	zone	shooter	run
shot	roll	block	slide
hook	defense	gym	toss
foul	offense	basket	hoop
travel			

TRACK TERMS:

hurdles	sand	speed	slow
broad jump	high jump	disqualify	burst
relay	cross country	default	kick
shot put	discus	swift	lanes
javelin	100 yard dash	perform	runner
pole vault	race	walk	starting gun
start	false start	chalk	cool
sprint	uniform	blocks	hot
baton	asphalt	fast	

Follow-Up Activity: Provide the following basketball and track "clothes" words for the student who is using other basketball and track terms. Ask him/her to read and define these words. Each time s/he succeeds, the student keeps that item of clothing. The object is to see how many sets of clothes a student can collect.

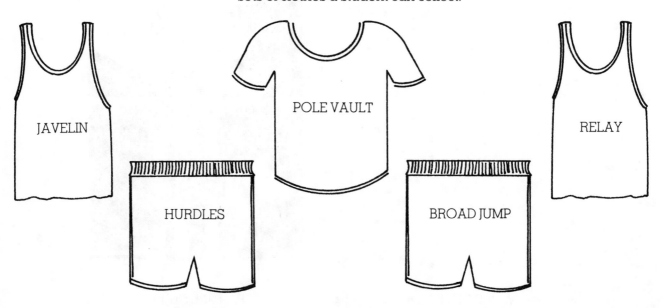

JAVELIN

POLE VAULT

RELAY

HURDLES

BROAD JUMP

Reeling in Words

Sport: Fishing

Purpose: To develop a student's fluent word-recognition skills using fishing terms; to be able to complete the proper sequence of events to write a news story.

Materials: Pencil

Discussion: Many students have a great love for fishing. Parents and teachers can make good use of fishing terms and related events to expand a student's word-recognition skills. The ability to sequence a story can help the student understand the order in which the events take place.

Directions: Present the following puzzle to the student. Have the student unscramble the words on the fish and write them in the blanks below. The first letter of each scrambled word is capitalized to help him/her recognize each scrambled word.

Answers, page 75

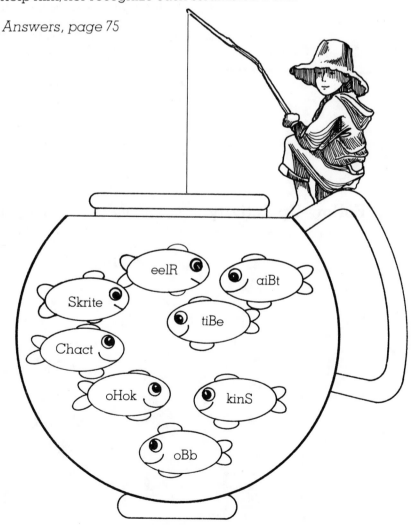

_____

_____

_____

_____

_____

_____

_____

Some additional fish terms to use in the unscrambling exercise:

rod	catfish	float	line
minnow	nibble	carp	worms
boat	drag	fly	perch
stringer	bass	trout	

Part 2 of this activity requires a youngster to read the following paragraph and complete the accompanying exercises:

Tom Wilson is a sports writer for the *Dallas Morning News*. He is writing a story of Jim Hall's big catch at last week's fishing competition. To help develop his article, Tom took notes. He finds these help him get the sequence of events right for his story.

Read each pair of Tom's sentences. Then circle the letter of the sentence that you think tells what happened first:

1. a. Jim Hall can <u>reel</u> in faster than anyone I know! His fish is enormous. What a beauty!
   b. Jim <u>baits</u> the hook then drops it in the water.

2. a. The line quickly <u>sinks</u> to the bottom.
   b. Jim <u>strikes</u> the fishing rod to set the hook.

3. a. With Jim's patience, he will <u>catch</u> a large fish.
   b. The fish is <u>hooked</u> now!

4. a. Jim hopes the fish will <u>bite</u> soon.
   b. The cork is <u>bobbing</u> in the water!

Answers, page 75

Follow-Up Activity: Rewrite the sentences from the previous activity in order, so they make one complete story.

Answers, page 76

Classy Stuff

Sport: Football

Purpose: To develop a student's comprehension by organizing and classifying ideas.

Materials: Paper, pencil, list of football terms

Discussion: Comprehension occurs when one can relate and organize what s/he reads to what is already known or experienced. One way to relate and group ideas is by classifying or categorizing information.

Directions: Give the student the following list of football terms and tell him/her to examine the list of words and explain what they all have in common.

Dallas Cowboys
helmet
fullback
shoulder pads
Pittsburgh Steelers
Washington Redskins
football
quarterback
tight end

Los Angeles Raiders
guard
Los Angeles Rams
jersey
linebacker
safety
Houston Oilers
defensive end
tackling dummy

When the student discovers that all the words relate to football, have him/her divide the terms into 3 smaller groups and ask what titles belong to each of these subdivisions.

GROUP I	GROUP II	GROUP III
title _____	title _____	title _____
_____	_____	_____
_____	_____	_____
_____	_____	_____
_____	_____	_____
_____	_____	_____
_____	_____	_____

Answers, page 76

Follow-Up Activity: Explain why each set of the following football-related terms can be grouped together. Then ask the student what category each group represents. See the example given.

---

title: *linemen*

5'11"-270 lbs   6'0"-260 lbs   5'9"-255 lbs   6'7"-285 lbs

---

1. title: _____

punt   place kick   kick off   field-goal attempt

2. title: _____

Jim Plunkett   Vince Ferragamo   Danny White

3. title: _____

fans   reporters   cheerleaders

4. title: _____

wishbone   shotgun   "I"

5. title: _____

touchdown   safety   field goal   extra points

6. title: _____

fullback   quarterback   halfback

7. title: _____

down-and-out   draw play   end around   pitch out

8. title: _____

Los Angeles Rams   Los Angeles Raiders

San Francisco 49'ers   San Diego Chargers

Answers, page 76

Running Wild—Imagination

Sport: Football

Purpose: To encourage students to use writing as a means of communication; to strengthen reading and writing skills.

Materials: Manila folder or a flat box such as a stationery box, an interesting picture of the sport of football, paste, pen, paper

Discussion: This activity will enable a parent or teacher to take advantage of a student's interest in a particular sport such as football to strengthen reading and writing skills.

Directions: Assuming the student already has some knowledge of football, prepare a writing kit as follows: On one side, inside a manila folder, paste a drawing or interesting picture illustrating some facet of football. Above the picture, write several possible story titles that might serve as creative writing stimulators for students. Opposite the picture, list numerous words which might be used in telling a story about the picture.

Tell the student that creating a football story stimulates knowledge and appreciation of the game. First, tell him/her to read all the titles above the picture and let his/her imagination go to work. Use the picture inside to develop a story about football. The words on the right side of the folder may help create more ideas for the student.

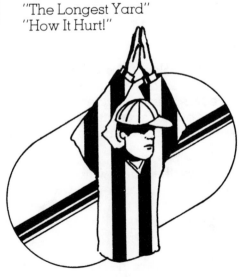

"Safety"
"The Wrong Call"
"Too Close for Comfort"
"The Longest Yard"
"How It Hurt!"

pass	first down
huddle	guard
blitz	receiver
completion	interception
coach	pile
referee	coin toss
tackle	nailed
blocking	defense
TD	offense
touchdown	extra points
safety	champion
field goal	score
tight end	screen pass
quarterback	forward pass
NFL	yard line
AFL	helmet
pushed back	offside
scrambling	onside kick
out-of-bounds	clip
punter	pursuit

If a flat box is used rather than the manila folder to construct the writing kit, place the picture and titles on the inside of the box lid. The list of words is written on the bottom of the box itself. Paper and pens are also included in the kit.

"Cracked Helmet"
"Ouch! Hurt on the Bench"
"The Quarterback Who Lost His Touch"

eligible receiver	clip
ineligible receiver	offside
in motion	holding
interference	kickoff
delay of game	time-out
penalty marker	pushing
playbook	tackle
unbeaten	yardage
injury	flag
plunge	field judge
diving	center
shoulder pads	cleats
hip pads	boundary
jerseys	blitz
fumble	blocking
signals	hand-off
official	foul

Follow-Up Activity:

Create other sports writing kits using sports in which the student is interested. S/he may even enjoy making kits. After the story is written, let the student share reading it with friends or adults. Some of these stories may be good vehicles to get a student involved in role-playing activities. The following football story is an example of one that would be fun for a student to act out:

"THE MIRACLE GAME"

The football season was all but over. Neither the Battlestars nor the Roughrunners had lost a game during the season. Now it was a chance to meet each other to decide the championship for the season. Tension was building on both teams. They knew in order to win the game a team could not make many mistakes.

The crowd cheered the 2 teams as they jogged onto the playing field. After the coin toss, the teams were ready for the first play of the game. The Battlestars' offensive unit was on the field since they had elected to receive the ball. David Sheffield caught the kickoff and ran it up to the 40-yard line. The Battlestars were off to a galloping start!

Art Jackson, the quarterback of the Battlestars, called the next play, "10-8-2," and made the handoff to O. J. Reeves. Reeves was one of the team's halfbacks and had been a star player for 4 years.

When O. J. got the ball, he put out all the speed he could muster. The fans were going crazy cheering. O. J. had managed to sail across the goal line just before being tackled by one of the Roughrunner players. He suddenly realized, however, that the game was being played in the Roughrunners' stadium. That huge, roaring cheer was coming from Roughrunner fans. When O. J. looked around, instead of seeing his teammates jumping for joy, he saw their heads hanging and the scorekeeper marking 2 points for the Roughrunners. The Roughrunners had scored a safety with O. J's run. He had carried the ball across the Battlestars' own goal.

The Roughrunners took possession of the ball. After 5 plays, they had moved the ball all the way to the Battlestar 4-yard line. The coach signaled to Charles Franks, the team's quarterback, to take a time-out. This would give them one minute in the huddle to plan their next important move. The referee blew the whistle; the time-out was over. Charles called the play and took the snap from the center. He dropped back to throw a pass. Suddenly the ball seemed to just slip out of his hand. In a super effort, Charles scrambled to get the ball before it reached the ground. By this time, the defensive players were rushing in like a plague. Charles tossed the ball toward the Battlestar goal where it was caught by Bruno Zezzappi for a touchdown. It was really a touchdown "on a shoestring" in more ways than one.

With only 15 seconds left to play in the game, the score was 16–10 in favor of the Roughrunners. They had really proven to be "the champs" of the season. The Battlestars had the ball, but they were back at their own 10-yard line. Quarterback Jackson stopped the clock for a last time-out. The Battlestar players certainly looked weary as they trudged to the huddle for the last time.

Back ready to make the last play, Jackson called out, "4-6-3." As he took the snap from the center, he dropped back in a last-ditch effort to make a pass. Just as he let go of the ball, a Roughrunner player collided with the ball to knock it off course and up in the air. The Battlestar fans started to leave because they knew their chances were over now for sure. Just at that moment, the crowd sounded one big gasp. The stray ball came down right into the hand of Art Jackson. Both teams were taken by surprise as Art caught his own pass and ran down the field for the TD. The final score was 17–16. Art's terrific pass had won the game.

Sequencing

Sport: Football

Purpose: To develop a student's comprehension of specific details by sequencing ideas from a story.

Materials: Paper, pencil

Discussion: Often at school, students are required to sequence ideas from their reading experiences for purposes of discussion, writing reports, or taking tests. This improves their overall understanding and recall of details as they appear in an article or story.

Directions: Ask the student to read the following statements silently. Afterwards, direct him/her to number each sentence in the order in which it would most likely appear to make a complete story in the following example.

_4_	The pass was completed.
_1_	Number 10 threw the ball.
_2_	The ball was flying through the air.
_3_	Number 19 caught the ball.

A.   ____ Johnny placed the football on a tee.
____ Johnny kicked the ball.
____ The field goal was good.
____ Johnny ran up to the ball.

B.   ____ The referee blew his whistle.
____ Jim was tackled on the 40-yard line.
____ Sam ran after Jim.
____ The ball was hiked.

C.   ____ Sam caught the ball.
____ The ball was passed to Sam.
____ Sam crossed the goal line.
____ Sam scored.

D.   ____ Mike had one minute left to make a touchdown.
____ The buzzer went off and the game was over.
____ Mike passed the ball to David who was on the 2-yard line.
____ David ran between 2 defensive players for the touchdown.

Answers, page 76

Follow-Up Activity: Ask the student to number the following pictures in the correct order that they might appear in a story. Place the numbers 1-6 to the left of each picture. Next, ask the student to write a caption for these pictures on the line beneath each one.

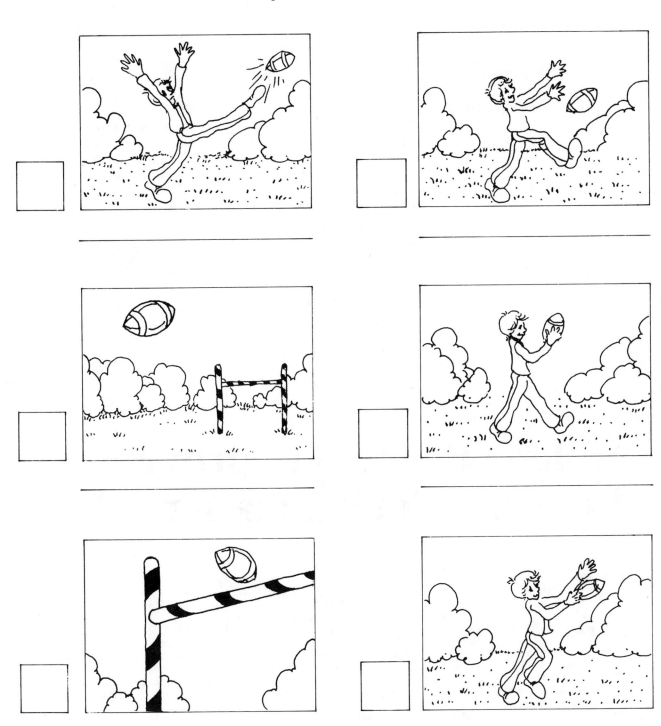

Answers, page 76

Will He Do It _nc_ More?

Sport: Golf

Purpose: To develop a student's ability to recognize long and short vowel sounds at the beginning, in the middle, and at the end of words.

Materials: Paper, pencils

Discussion: Because many students are interested in sports and motivated to read sports-related newspaper or magazine articles, these can be used to strengthen their understanding of long and short vowel sounds. By using a "cloze" activity (fill-in-the-blanks), parents and teachers can strengthen youngsters' recognition of the vowels as they appear in words and encourage them to practice writing these in their proper form.

Directions: Have the student read the following article. Then present the following cloze exercises to the student in which the vowels have been omitted from some of the words. In order to complete the exercise, s/he must supply the vowels that are missing. Allow sufficient time to complete the exercise. See the example below.

He is called the G_old_en Bear.

Golden Bear out to prove PGA's no joking matter

By Sam Blair
Staff Writer of The News

DULUTH, Ga.—Funny how hard times inspire wisecracks. When Jack Nicklaus shot an 83 in the British Open, radio commentator Paul Harvey said, "I always wanted to play golf like Jack Nicklaus. Now I do."

OK, maybe the Golden Bear left a little notoriety at Royal St. George's but that doesn't mean he's not a dadgum hero around heah, boy. Why, he's won the PGA championship five times. Last year at Oak Hill he didn't just capture it. He imprisoned it. Won by seven strokes and left the rest playing for second.

Now they're ready to tee it up Thursday on Atlanta AC's Highlands course, a 7,070-yard layout for long hitters. Nicklaus has to be one of the favorites even if he hasn't won a major championship this year, or rarely shown signs of taking charge like he did last summer at the PGA and U.S. Open. Can he find his tonic out there on those sweltering acres by the Chattahoochee River?

If he does, it will be a real blast from the past. A sixth PGA title will make Jack alone at the top of the champions' list, one up on Walter Hagen, who used to wipe up the field a couple of generations back when this one was match play.

Dallas Morning News (Aug 6, 1981)
Answers, page 77

Funny how hard times __nsp__r__ wisecracks. When Jack Nicklaus sh__t an 83 in the Br__t__sh Open, radio commentator Paul H__rv__y said, "I always wanted t__ play golf like Jack N__ckl__ __s. Now I do."

OK, m__yb__ the Golden Bear left a L__ttl__ notoriety at Royal St. G__ __rg__'s but that doesn't mean h__'s not a dadgum hero __r__ __nd heah, boy. Why, he's w__n the PGA championship five t__m__s. Last year at Oak H__ll he didn't just capture __t. He imprisoned it. Won b__ seven strokes and left th__ rest playing for second.

N__w they're ready to t__ __ it up Thursday on __tl__nt__ AC's Highlands course, a 7,070-y__rd layout for long hitters. N__ckl__ __s has to be one __f the favorites even if h__ hasn't won a major ch__mp__ __nsh__p this year, or rarely sh__wn signs of taking charge L__k__ he did last summer __t the PGA and U.S. __p__n. Can he find his t__n__c out there on those sw__lt__r__ng acres by the Chattahooche R__v__r?

If he does, it w__l be a real blast fr__m the past. A sixth PG__ title will make Jack __l__n__e at the top of the ch__mp__ __ns' list, one up on W__lt__r Hagen, who used to w__p__ __p the field a c__ __pl__ of g__n__r__t__ __ns back when this one was m__tch play.

Answers, page 77

Follow-Up Activity: Reinforce the recognition of vowel sounds by presenting the words listed below which are taken from the previous newspaper article. Ask the student to supply words whose vowel sounds rhyme with the word in the box at the top of each column in the blanks below each word.

ring	blast	jail	map	grab
sing	*mast*	*hail*	*clap*	*tab*

Will He Do It __nc__ More?

coat	page	find	real	shown
goat	*wage*	*kind*	*deal*	*thrown*

Answers, page 77

Doing the Splits
with Prefixes and Suffixes

Sport: Gymnastics

Purpose: To develop a student's ability to recognize words with the following prefixes and suffixes (dis, re, er, ing, ed, es, s, less).

Materials: 2 envelopes, numerous blank cards

Discussion: Print terms related to gymnastics on small cards to teach a student to recognize new words by adding prefixes and suffixes to a base (root) word. The ability to use both prefixes and suffixes effectively demonstrates the difference between strong and weak word-recognition skill.

Directions: Develop a "root words" envelope like the one illustrated in this activity and ask the student to select a root word. Then make up a "prefixes and suffixes" envelope and ask him/her to choose a prefix or suffix from it. Using the enclosed illustration as a guide, ask the student to place the root word on one side of the center line and the prefix or suffix on the other. Tell the student that the object of the exercise is to create a real word by combining the root word with a prefix or suffix. For example: you will notice the root word "jump" appears to the left of the line and the suffix "ing" stands to. the right.

JUMP	ING

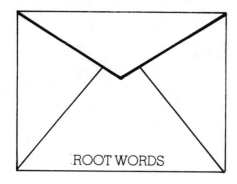

For the root words envelope:

side horse	exercise	push	approach
balance	gymnast	extend	warm up
practice	tumble	stretch	stunt
win	bar	body	spot
coach	arm	toe	mat
point	leg	jump	routine
swing	score	spring	floor
squat	cartwheel	hop	flip
kick	compete	leap	train
footstep	roll	perform	call
award	roundoff	vault	judge
medal	mount	pose	tire

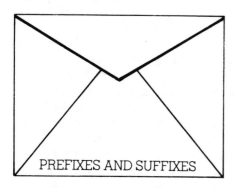

For the prefixes and the suffixes envelope:

dis	er	ed	es
re	ing	less	s

Follow-Up Activity:

Have the student complete the following multiple-choice activity with his/her new words. Ask him/her to underline the correct answer.

1. Gymnasts put rosin on their feet to keep them from slipping when (vault, vaulted, vaulting).

2. A (spot, spotter, spotting) is a person who stands nearby so s/he can catch the gymnast in case of a fall.

3. Be sure you have enough (mat, mats, matted) for proper protection.

4. One must (mounts, mounting, dismount) when coming off the balance beam.

5. The gymnast will be (approaching, approached, approaches) the uneven parallel bars soon.

6. The coach gave his star athlete an important toe (pointer, pointed, pointless).

7. Nadia will be (practices, practicing, practiced) 4 hours a day, 6 days a week for the competition.

8. The gymnasts were (recalled, calling, calls) to the auditorium for the awards ceremony.

9. The gymnast seemed (tiring, tires, tireless) in the long performance.

10. When Olga (extending, extends, extend) her body as far as possible, it is (stretching, stretched, stretches) to its full length.

11. Olga can (relive, relived, reliving) her days of triumph.

12. When Nadia began to fall, the spotter (reacted, react, reacting).

13. Nadia was (disinterested, disinterest, disinteresting) in the countryside scenery because her mind was on her next performance.

14. When Olga lost to Nadia, she was (disappoint, disappointing, disappointed).

15. Olga was beginning to (disliking, disliked, dislike) Nadia.

Answers, page 77

A Barrel of Words and Ideas

Sport: Rodeo

Purpose: To develop a student's sight vocabulary and increase comprehension (Sight vocabulary words are generally words that cannot be read phonetically.).

Materials: A number of paper cones or cylinders—(these may be obtained from large, commercial size rolls of string or bath and kitchen paper products), paper strips or 3" × 5" index cards, small plastic horse or cut-out shape of a horse, tape or tacks, pen

Discussion: The skill of recognizing sight words instantly is important for a student's growth in reading. Many of these words form the basis of all written material.

Directions: Prepare 3" × 5" cards or paper strips with the following sight words written on the front side. Include a different variety depending on the age or reading level of the student.

steer	calf	lure
leather	chute	thrown
bronc	Brahma	trample
danger	vicious	surcingle

On the back side of the card or paper strip, write a sentence in which the word is used.

Event

front side of card

It was the first event.

back side of card

56

Tack or tape one or 2 word/sentence strips to each cone. Set the cones in the same way barrels are arranged for barrel racing in rodeo (placed in groups of 3). Unlike actual rodeo, however, several groups of 3 barrels each will be needed to accommodate this activity. The arrows beginning in front of the horse indicate the path the horse should take to complete the activity.

Explain to the student that s/he is going to help the horse through the race by reading the words and sentences on the barrels correctly. The student directs the horse around the barrels in the manner illustrated by removing the strip or 3" × 5" card from each barrel by loosening the tacks or removing the tape. After the student reads the strip or strips attached to a particular barrel, the horse may then proceed around it. If a student cannot successfully read the word or sentence, the barrel is "knocked over."

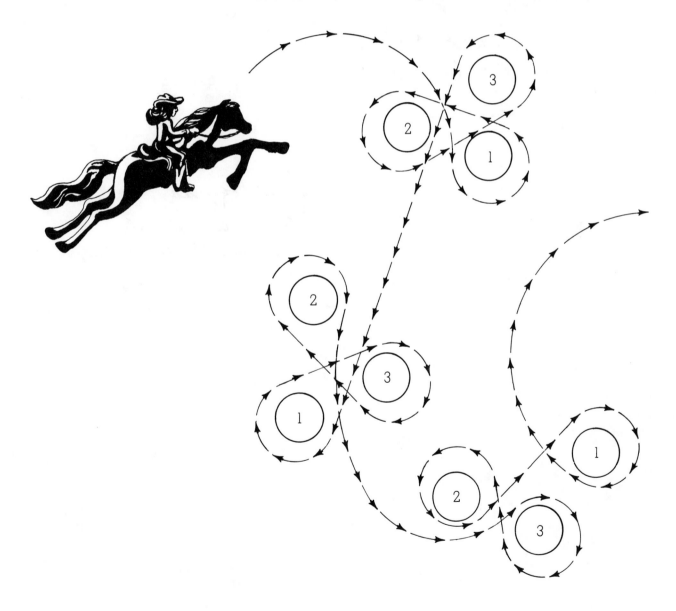

Follow-Up Activity: Using the format employed in the initial barrel race, write a literal comprehension question on the front of a paper strip which is based on a youngster's reading assignment. Write 3 or 4 answer choices on the back side of the paper strip—you may wish to put the page number on each strip where the student can check his/her answer. Tell the youngster prior to the reading of an assignment that s/he should remember as much as possible because the information will help the student through the barrel race. As the student correctly answers the questions, s/he progresses through the "barrel race" course.

Question:
Bareback riding
is similar to
_____?

front of paper strip

a. Bulldogging
b. Bronc riding
c. Brahma bull riding
page 43

back of paper strip

Contract Skating

Sport: Skating

Purpose: To develop a student's word recognition by introducing him/her to contractions.

Materials: Paper, pencil

Discussion: Contractions are often found in a student's reading material. It is important that the student recognize a contraction as a shortened form of 2 words so that s/he can apply the proper meaning.

Directions: Discuss the meaning of the contractions in the first list below with the student. Then ask the youngster to read the paragraphs that follow and choose, from the second list of contractions, the one that completes each sentence. Tell him/her that some of the contractions may be used more than once.

don't—do not	they've—they have
can't—can not	you'll—you will
it's—it is	there's—there is
I'm—I am	you've—you have
it'll—it will	won't—will not

you've	you're	there's	it's
don't	they've	don'ts	it'll
you'll	can't	I'm	can'ts
won't			

Many people _____ believe how easy skating can really be. They make statements like "I _____ know how to skate," I _____ do that," or "_____ too clumsy. But once _____ learned how to skate, the "_____" seem to disappear. _____ like learning to ride a bike; once _____ learned how to skate _____ never forget!

It takes practice to learn the basics of skating. Of course, _____ a list of do's and _____ to follow, but once _____ mastered them _____ have no problems. Just remember that _____ learning a new sport and _____ take time for you to become a pro. But if _____ take it one step at a time, it _____ take you long to learn how to skate with great confidence.

Answers, page 78

Follow-Up Activity: Ask the student to match each contraction in the left column by drawing a line to the 2 words in the right column that form the contraction.

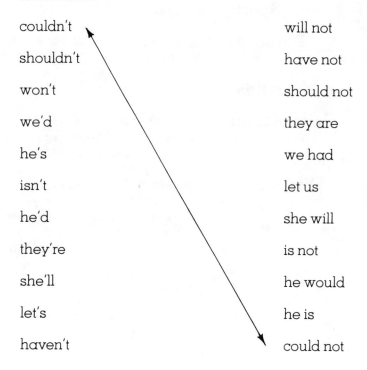

couldn't	will not
shouldn't	have not
won't	should not
we'd	they are
he's	we had
isn't	let us
he'd	she will
they're	is not
she'll	he would
let's	he is
haven't	could not

An Old Sport

Sport: Soccer

Purpose To expand a student's use of structural-analysis skills by introducing a number of activities on words found in a soccer-related sports story.

Material: Pencils, paper, soccer-related story

Discussion: Parents and teachers can make good use of sports-related newspaper or magazine articles to teach students various structural-analysis skills such as word syllables, prefixes, suffixes, roots, compounds, and contractions. The above-mentioned skills may be used to increase a student's ability to recognize a large store of previously unknown words.

Directions: Using the following sports story, have the student underline all words that have suffixes and prefixes—words that have meaningful elements attached to the beginning (prefix) or end (suffix). When the student has finished (allow approximately 10 minutes for completion of the exercise), have the student make a list of words underlined. Assist the student with any difficulties s/he may have.

Silvio leads Tornado to 3–1 win

By Steve Tracy
Staff Writer of The News

Silvio's 2-goal performance spoiled Texas Tech product and Washington goalie Jim Messemer's NASL debut as Dallas handled the Diplomats, 3-1, at Texas Stadium Friday night.

The win is Dallas' third in four starts

■ **Tornado may move to different stadium. Page 2B**

after snapping a NASL record 20-game losing streak and the Tornado's second straight, but coach Peter Short pointed to a statistic more significant.

"This is the first time we have come from behind to win," said Short of the Tornado, down 1-0 at halftime. "This is something the team hasn't seen, which shows a new aggressiveness . . . an indication of a new spirit."

Silvio, the young leftwing from Brazil, scored his first two goals of the season. Both came in the second half against Messemer, who was making the first start of his professional career. He was replacing Jim Brown, who was sidelined with tendinitis. Messemer was the Dips' second-round draft pick after four years in goal for Texas Tech.

"The rookie (Messemer) played a great first half," Short said, "and handled some very difficult shots, but I think his inexperience showed in the second half, especially on Rausch's goal."

Off a pass from Silvio, right wing Wolfgang Rausch kicked one from 10-feet out that went right through Messemer's legs to tie the game, 1-1, at 67:05.

"It was an off-speed shot by Rausch," Short said, "and I think that really threw him off."

Three minutes later, Silvio booted in a 30-yarder past Messemer for his first score of the season, unassisted, with 69:57 gone for Dallas' first lead and then beat Washington defenders off a feed from Rausch at 88:04 for the final goal.

"Our first goal, while well engineered, was lucky," Short said "although Silvo's two goals were great. He's young . . . full of running.

"Our play tonight was more aggressive, which is what we are trying to achieve," Short said. "Our first half, we were a little anxious, but then in the second, we started attacking very well."

The Diplomats' loss was the third in a row for the team that is fighting for a NASL playoff berth.

"Injuries are hurting us . . . causing some major problems in our game," Washington coach Ken Furby said of the injured, now totaling half the team roster. "And we weren't aggressive tonight . . . the heat hurt to an extent with a good first half followed by a poor second."

Dallas Morning News (July 29, 1981)
Answers, page 78

The following list of words are taken from the newspaper article. Using the space provided, write the root word, any suffix, or any prefix for each word in the list.

		ROOT WORD	SUFFIX	PREFIX
a.	performance			
b.	spoiled			
c.	leads			
d.	handled			
e.	different			
f.	snapping			
g.	losing			
h.	pointed			
i.	aggressiveness			
j.	indication			
k.	scored			
l.	tendinitis			
m.	making			
n.	professional			
o.	replacing			
p.	rookie			
q.	played			
r.	especially			
s.	really			
t.	booted			
u.	anxious			
v.	unassisted			

Answers, page 78

Follow-Up Activity

Have the student identify the 6 compound words in the list below (taken from the preceding article about soccer) and write them in the blanks provided

totaling	causing	injuries	running
tonight	offspeed	halftime	something
engineered	hurting	sidelined	trying
playoff	fighting	attacking	aggressive
lucky	inexperience	started	leftwing

COMPOUND WORDS

1. _____

2. _____

3. _____

4. _____

5. _____

6. _____

Answers, page 79

Soccer Can Be Puzzling

Sports: Soccer

Purpose: To develop a student's ability to read and locate information and apply it in a different context.

Materials: Prepared soccer puzzle, pencil, and paper

Discussion: Parents and teachers can use a story related to soccer and a crossword puzzle to teach a student some of the terminology of the game.

Directions: Present the following story and puzzle about soccer to the student. After reading the story, have the student provide the correct words in the blank spaces of the puzzle.

The fastest growing sport in America today is soccer. Children often use any rubber ball to play the game but usually a regular soccer ball is used. Soccer is played on a large field. Eleven players are on each team. The idea of the game is to advance the ball using one's feet, head, shoulders, and legs up or down the field toward a goal. If a player breaks a rule during the game, a foul is called by the referee. Very little equipment is worn since players need a lot of freedom to move about quickly. However, shoes, shirt, shorts, socks, and shin guards are the basic uniform.

ACROSS:

1. What players wear on their feet
2. A mistake in soccer
4. What one does with a ball
6. Number of players on a team

DOWN:

1. The fastest growing sport
2. The place where a soccer game is played
3. A player kicks a _____
5. Eleven players are on a

_____

Answers, page 79

Variation: Place one set of sports terms (all hockey, basketball, etc.) on a circular disc with a metal or cardboad arrow fastened in the center. Each contestant spins the arrow. When the arrow stops spinning, it will be pointing at a word on the wheel. Match the word closest to the point of the arrow with the same word used in a sentence from a prepared list of sentences. See the example below:

The black team was awarded a free <u>kick.</u>

SOCCER WHEEL:

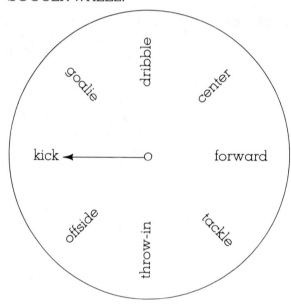

1. The forward passed the ball to the center forward.

2. The game begins in the center of the field.

3. A good soccer player can dribble down the field without losing stride or the ball.

4. When a soccer player is offside, a penalty is called.

5. When the ball goes out, there must be a throw-in.

6. The goalie saved the game when he caught the ball.

7. In soccer the player does more than just kick the ball.

8. To tackle an opponent in soccer, one must get the ball away.

Follow-Up Activity:

Discuss the following terms on the left side of the page with the student. Indicate how they are used by referring to the diagram below. Afterwards, ask the student to match the terms on the left with the definitions on the right:

forward   not enough opponents between you and the goalie

goalie box   the player on the front line

goalie   kicking the ball to a teammate

fullback   the place on the field where the game starts

circle   the area that is the goalie's responsibility

throw-in   the player who helps the goalie

offside   the player who defends the goal

passing   to put the ball into play from the sidelines

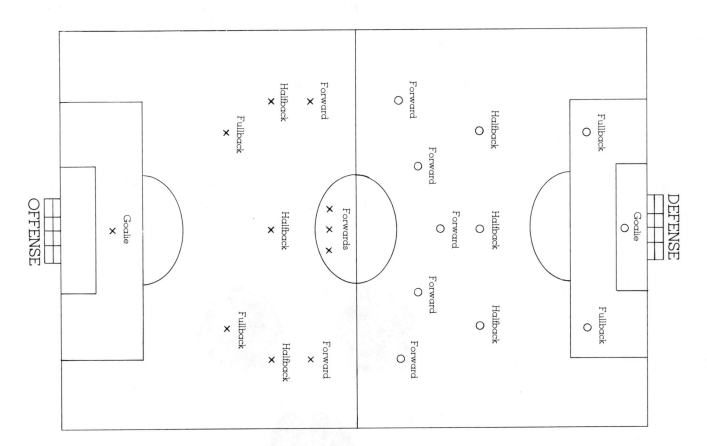

Answers, page 79

Soccer Suffixes

Sport: Soccer

Purpose: To develop a student's discrimination of the verb tenses by identifying the suffixes ed and ing.

Materials: White construction paper, black marker, metal paper brad, scissors, soccer-related terms

Discussion: Parents and teachers can use a device that looks like a soccer ball and makes use of soccer terms to motivate a student's discrimination and recognition of verb tense suffixes. These endings play an important roll in language by changing the time in which the action of a verb occurs; therefore, it is necessary to recognize and understand such suffixes.

Directions: Cut 2 circles out of construction paper, one 6" in diameter and the other 7" in diameter. Center the smaller circle on top of the larger and fasten in the middle with a brad. The smaller circle should rotate freely on top of the larger. Decorate the smaller circle to look like a soccer ball and write the following verbs as shown on the diagram:

center	pass	roll
kick	loft	sprint
head	block	butt

On the larger circle on the right hand side, print the suffixes ed and ing as in the diagram.

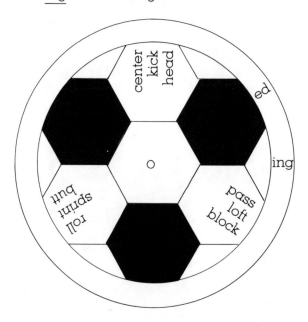

66

Give the illustrated soccer ball to the student and have him/her match the suffixes on the outside with a verb written on the inside. First, have the student read the verb without either suffix. Then have the student read the verb with both suffixes. Explain to him/her how the change in suffix affects the time sequence in which the action of the verb takes place, i.e., by adding the suffix ed the action of the verb has taken place in the past, and by adding ing the action of the verb is ongoing.

Follow-Up Activity: Fill in the blanks with the word choice that makes sense in each sentence.

1. The center _____ a goal.
    (score, scored, scoring)

2. The halfback _____ the ball.
    (trap, trapped, trapping)

3. A player _____ the ball down the field.
    (dribble, dribbled, dribbling)

4. A soccer player must be able to _____ quickly.
    (stop, stopped, stopping)

5. The player is _____ the ball from the corner.
    (kick, kicked, kicking)

6. The fans _____ very loudly at all the games.
    (yell, yelled, yelling)

7. That player will _____ to the center.
    (pass, passed, passing)

8. That goal was scored by _____ the ball.
    (head, headed, heading)

9. The player _____ the ball to set up the goal.
    (center, centered, centering)

10. Those players are _____ down the field.
    (sprint, sprinted, sprinting)

11. The halfback _____ the ball into the air.
    (loft, lofted, lofting)

12. The goalie must try to _____ all goal attempts.
    (block, blocked, blocking)

Answers, page 79

Reading High Jumper

Sport: Track and Field

Purpose: To extend a student's sight word vocabulary and give practice with those words s/he may already know.

Materials: A list of the following sight words related to track and field events ranging from easy to more difficult levels, index cards, crayon pens, photocopy of reading high jump boards provided in this activity, photocopies of ribbons that should then be colored green, yellow, red, and blue

Discussion: Sight words are words that a student can recognize immediately without phonic analysis. In order for a student to become a fluid reader, the student must develop a large sight-word vocabulary. Because many students are highly interested in sports, the words from different games and events can be used to teach a variety of sight words.

Directions: From the sight-word list below, prepare index cards with a sight word printed on each. Along with each sight word, copy the number adjacent to each sight word on the index card. The number indicates the relative level of difficulty for each sight word—one for the easier words to 3 for the most difficult. The numbers will be used to chart the student's ability to recognize sight words. For each word correctly recognized, the student scores the value indicated for that word. The game continues until either s/he progresses through all the cards or fails to identify 7 consecutive sight words. When the game is completed, ribbons are awarded based on the student's total score. A green ribbon is given to the student who has accumulated 15–35 points; a yellow ribbon for 36–55 points; a red ribbon for 56–75 points; and a blue ribbon for any number of points above 76.

leap (2)	win (1)	hurdle (3)	run (1)
set(1)	lose (2)	sprint (3)	field (3)
ready (2)	discus (3)	hop (1)	pole (1)
distance (3)	meters (3)	skip (2)	broad (2)
mile (2)	long (2)	tape (2)	fall (1)
yards (2)	speed (2)	event (3)	line (2)
trip (2)	uniform (3)	put (1)	race (1)
stadium (3)	lead (2)	sweat (2)	lane (2)
start (2)	baton (3)	hurt (1)	walk (3)
finish (3)	jump (2)	injury (3)	throw (3)
blocks·(3)	fast (2)	track (2)	hammer (3)
spikes (3)			

READING HIGH JUMPER AWARDS

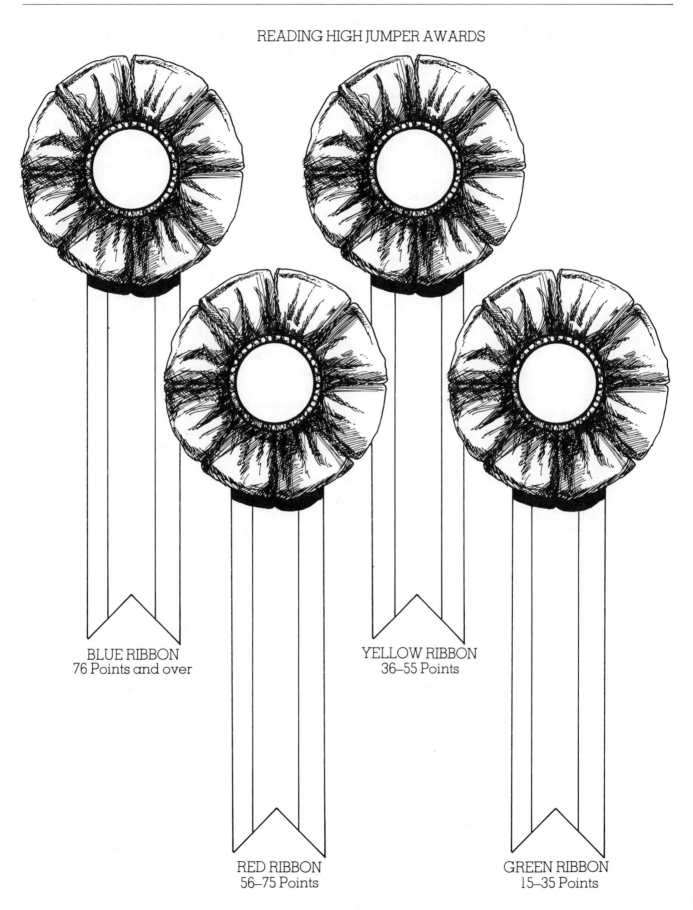

BLUE RIBBON
76 Points and over

YELLOW RIBBON
36–55 Points

RED RIBBON
56–75 Points

GREEN RIBBON
15–35 Points

Follow-Up Activity: Read and discuss the use of each word read incorrectly during the preceding game. Develop sentences using the words missed, but leave blanks instead of writing the track and field sight words to be studied. Next to each sentence, give possible choices in parentheses. Have students write the correctly spelled answers in the blanks. Examples are provided below:

1. There was one _____ during the races, but no one was hurt badly. (engery, injury)

2. The next _____ is the high jump. (event, avint)

3. It is more fun to win than to _____. (loose, lose)

4. The _____ is about to start. (rase, race)

5. I like to go to a _____ meet. (track, trak)

6. It is time to run the 100 _____ dash. (yrad, yard)

7. In _____ races, the runners race for less than 220 yards. (sprit, sprint)

8. The _____ was filled with people. (stadium, stadeum)

9. In a relay race, the runners on each team hand each other a _____. (button, baton)

10. He set a record for the longest _____ jump. (braud, broad)

11. She was _____ to begin the race at the starting line. (ready, redy)

12. You must learn how to spin the _____ so it will glide. (discuss, discus)

13. He cleared all the _____. (hurdles, hurddles)

14. Most runners wear _____. (sprieks, spikes)

15. They _____ a heavy metal ball in the shot put event. (through, throw)

16. He dropped the baton as he crossed the _____ line. (finish, finnich)

17. She set a record for the fastest _____. (speed, spede)

18. The uniform was wet with _____. (sweet, sweat)

19. He had the _____ in the race. (leed, lead)

20. The _____ he had run was 50 yards. (distance, distenc)

Answers, page 79

Answers to Elementary Section

Get Equipped! Reading Olympics

1. *RACQUETBALL RACQUET*
2. *SKI VEST*
3. *COMBO WATER SKIS*
4. *BASKETBALL SHOE*
5. BASEBALL GLOVE
6. TENNIS RACQUETS
7. **motocross bicycle**
8. **SOCCER SHOE**
9. *LEG WEIGHT*
10. **BASEBALL CAP**
11. **BASKETBALL**
12. *GOLF CLUB*
13. *TENNIS SHOE*
14. **soccer ball**

Wanted! Heroes and Heroines!

RACE TRACK PUZZLE

1. racing
2. gymnastics
3. boxing
4. football
5. ice hockey
6. baseball
7. basketball
8. soccer

Follow-Up Activity #1

BASKETBALL	FOOTBALL	BOXING	SOCCER
hoop	helmet	punch	forward
forward	forward	round	tackle
key	tackle	dancing	dribble
free throw	kickoff	center	throw-in
dribble	fumble	speed	offside
guard	first down	box	kick
center	kick	left hook	goalie
foul	touchdown	out cold	center
	guard	knockout	heading
	center	lightweight	speed
	speed		goalie
	fullback		heeling
			fullback
			foul
			penalty box

HOCKEY	BASEBALL	GYMNASTICS	STOCK CAR RACING
forward	helmet	stretch	helmet
race	race	cartwheel	race
helmet	pitcher	roundoff	tires
goalie	base	dancing	crew
center	double play	amplitude	grandstand
stick	home plate	dismount	mechanics
shot	strike	vault	speed
puck	center	balance	pit stop
foul	catcher	horse	track
penalty box	pop fly		lap
skates	fly ball		
rink	foul		

Seek and You Shall Find

1. rugby
2. bowling
3. hockey
4. tennis
5. volleyball
6. boxing
7. swimming
8. golf
9. soccer
10. baseball
11. football
12. track
13. fishing
14. basketball
15. wrestling

Follow-Up Activity

WORD SEARCH PUZZLE

y	b	g	u	r	f	s	d	q	l	d	c	l	t
o	f	p	n	l	d	l	c	m	l	b	l	a	r
c	d	e	x	l	o	m	b	f	a	a	r	w	j
g	i	t	r	a	c	k	s	o	b	x	n	p	q
n	o	v	s	b	b	d	f	t	t	t	o	m	h
i	b	o	g	e	s	b	o	l	e	i	g	t	o
h	f	l	n	s	h	o	l	n	k	b	n	v	c
s	u	l	i	a	f	a	n	r	s	d	i	w	k
i	b	e	x	b	b	i	o	p	a	z	l	k	e
f	d	y	o	p	s	o	d	c	b	p	t	m	y
b	s	b	b	g	n	i	m	m	i	w	s	z	r
a	t	a	z	h	o	d	s	o	c	c	e	r	a
c	m	l	b	o	w	l	i	n	g	l	r	s	d
e	n	l	r	t	c	h	f	t	n	a	w	m	p

Sports Analogies

A.	12	E.	11	I.	4
B.	9	F.	3	J.	6
C.	1	G.	2	K.	5
D.	7	H.	10	L.	8

Titles Away!

SUGGESTED TITLES

1. "Dallas: The Scene for Multisports"
2. "Punt, Pass, Kick to Pontiac"
3. "Rounding the Track"
4. "Shooting Star Adams"
5. "Ralph in the Open"

Follow-Up Activity

1. exercise
2. moved as one
3. a system of exercise
4. horse
5. the player by the basket
6. a score on a hole of one under par
7. a type of golf club—No. 1 wood
8. golfclub

Amazing Words from Baseball

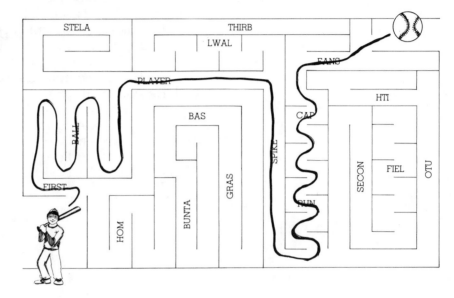

Getting It Together— Baseball Compounds
Follow-Up Activity

1. batboy
2. playoff
3. infield
4. shortstop
5. baseball
6. strikeout
7. outfield
8. fastball

Seek and Find: Baseball Words

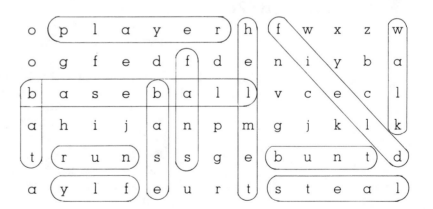

Speaking of Baseball

"Hey, Charlie! Give this guy one of your curveballs. Make the ball walk and talk as it comes over the plate," said Mac.

"Well, Mac, I don't think this guy is ready for that. You better offer him something to clean his glasses," answered Charlie.

"It won't do any good for him to clean his glasses. He will think he was dreaming when the ump calls him out. Man, you have him going your way. Strike him out!" responded Mac.

Charlie wound up and let the pitch go. It was a strike.

"It was all right, Charlie! That was strike one. You just need 2 more," yelled Mac.

Charlie sent another pitch straight across the plate.

"Great! Charlie, just one more," hollered Mac.

"Mac, clean off the plate so I can throw a real curve. This is going to be an easy out!" yelled Charlie.

Charlie threw but it was not a strike. The ball sailed by just inches from the batter's eyes. Even the fans knew before the ump made the call that it was a ball.

"Charlie, settle down! You only need one good spin and you have him," counseled Mac.

"Okay, Mac. Here goes!" exclaimed Charlie.

The ball flew across the plate. However, the batter hit a foul ball. He started cursing.

Charlie knew he had the batter now. He wound up for the last time. It was a perfect pitch! The batter swung with all his might and missed. He left the plate wishing he'd never seen a baseball.

Of course Charlie left the mound in a state of joy. He had helped his team win the state championship.

"You should feel real proud, Charlie," cried Mac.

Follow-Up Activity #1

1. M	5. M	8. C
2. M	6. M	9. C
3. C	7. M	10. M
4. M		

Follow-Up Activity #2

1. said	4. yelled	7. counseled
2. answered	5. hollered	8. exclaimed
3. responded	6. yelled	9. cried

A Sports Zoo

SENTENCES

1. eagle-eyed—to watch sharply
2. cocky—pert; arrogant
3. snake in the grass—a faithless friend
4. dog-tired—fatigued; extremely weary
5. outfoxed—outsmarted
6. catcalls—a noise made to express disapproval
7. bullheaded—stubborn
8. horsing around—not paying attention; rough play
9. hogging—to take more than one's share
10. skunked—to defeat an opponent by more than doubling their score; to be shut out in a game

Follow-Up Activity

A. 8	E. 1	H. 4
B. 6	F. 3	I. 5
C. 7	G. 10	J. 2
D. 9		

Free Throw

Americans defeat Soviets in double-OT

By GIL LeBRETON
Star-Telegram Writer

BUCHAREST, Romania—A wild U.S.-Soviet semifinal in the World University Games basketball tournament overshadowed record-setting gold medal performances at the track and swimming pool Saturday as the flashy Americans downed the Soviets, 113-107, in double-overtime.

A mostly Romanian crowd of about 1,600 turned the tiny Giulesti gymnasium into a hotbox, cheering the moves of Villanova's John Pinone and LSU's Howard Carter as well as some hotly contested officials' calls that went against the Soviets.

But empty seats were abundant at the 70,000-capacity track stadium, while spectators tried to squeeze past security guards into the gym where Americans and Soviets clashed on the basketball court.

Carter scored 28 points, most of them from the outside, and Pinone collected 27, many against 7-foot-4 Soviet center Vladimir Tkachenko under the basket.

John Bagley of Boston College, Kevin Boyle of Iowa and Kevin Magee of California-Irvine worked an acrobatic inside offense against the big Soviets, and combined with North Carolina State's Sid Lowe to shake up the Soviets on defense.

"Our quickness bothers some people," said Coach Tom Davis of Boston College.

Soviet coach Vladimir Kolos and several Soviet players bitterly protested the officials' decisions that kept the Americans in the game.

With the score tied at 101 in the first overtime, a foul was called against the United States in a rebound battle under the Soviet basket. Officials at first signaled that the Soviets would get two free throws, but changed the decision seconds later, saying time had run out.

"Today the shots fell for us and didn't fall for them," said Davis.

Sergei Iovasa was the game's high scorer with 29 points for the Soviets.

Canada, which had handed the United States an 78-76 defeat the night before, beat Mexico, 81-67, and was undefeated going into its last semifinal round game against the Soviets Sunday.

homograph:
(to run on a track)
(top track an animal)
(to keep track of)

homograph:
(to eat a round steak)
(a 10-round boxing match)
(to gather round the fire)

Sentence content will vary. The meanings of the 10 words as they are used in the article are:

1. protest—complain
2. center—the player in the middle of the back 3 players, normally the one who takes the jump-ball when the ball is held by both teams.
3. combine—joined together
4. game—basketball
5. points—a number earned by a player indicating the number of successful shots.
6. defense—strategy employed by the team without the ball.
7. offense—strategy employed by the team with possession of the ball.
8. contest—to raise questions about an event
9. court—the playing area for a basketball game
10. record—the highest achievement currently held in an event.

Follow-Up Activity

1. home
2. fans
3. ball
4. five
5. two
6. period
7. jump
8. referee

MYSTERY WORD: halftime

Reeling in Words

eelR - reel
aiBt - bait
Skrite - strike

tiBe - bite
kinS - sink
Chact - catch

oHok - hook
oBb-bob

1. b
2. a
3. a
4. a

Follow-Up Activity SEQUENCED STORY

Jim baits the hook then drops it in the water. The line, quickly sinks to the bottom. Jim hopes the fish will bite soon. With Jim's patience, he will catch a large fish. The cork is bobbing in the water! Jim strikes the fishing rod to set the hook. The fish is hooked now! Jim Hall can reel in faster than anyone I know! His fish is enormous. What a beauty!

Classy Stuff

TEAMS	EQUIPMENT	PLAYERS
Dallas Cowboys	helmet	fullback
Pittsburgh Steelers	shoulder pads	quarterback
Washington Redskins	football	tight end
Los Angeles Raiders	jersey	guard
Los Angeles Rams	tackling dummy	linebacker
Houston Oilers		safety
		defensive end

Follow-Up Activity STUDENTS' ANSWERS MAY VARY:

types of kicks	ways to score
names of quarterbacks	offensive backs
people attending the game	types of offensive plays
offensive formation	teams in California

Sequencing

A.	B.	C.	D.
1	4	2	1
3	3	1	4
4	2	3	2
2	1	4	3

Follow-Up Activity

4	3
5	1
6	2

Will He Do It __nc__ More?

Golden Bear out to prove PGA's no joking matter

By Sam Blair
Staff Writer of The News

DULUTH, Ga.—Funny how hard times inspire wisecracks. When Jack Nicklaus shot an 83 in the British Open, radio commentator Paul Harvey said, "I always wanted to play golf like Jack Nicklaus. Now I do."

OK, maybe the Golden Bear left a little notoriety at Royal St. George's but that doesn't mean he's not a dadgum hero around heah, boy. Why, he's won the PGA championship five times. Last year at Oak Hill he didn't just capture it. He imprisoned it. Won by seven strokes and left the rest playing for second.

Now they're ready to tee it up Thursday on Atlanta AC's Highlands course, a 7,070-yard layout for long hitters. Nicklaus has to be one of the favorites even if he hasn't won a major championship this year, or rarely shown signs of taking charge like he did last summer at the PGA and U.S. Open. Can he find his tonic out there on those sweltering acres by the Chattahoochee River?

If he does, it will be a real blast from the past. A sixth PGA title will make Jack alone at the top of the champions' list, one up on Walter Hagen, who used to wipe up the field a couple of generations back when this one was match play.

The underlined portions of these words represent the missing vowels in this student activity.

MISSING VOWEL SOUNDS OF SELECTED WORDS:

inspire shot British Harvey to Nicklaus maybe little George's he's around won times Hill it by the Now tee Atlanta yard Nicklaus of he championship shown like at Open tonic sweltering River will from PGA alone champions' Walter wipe couple generations match

Answers will vary. Accept any rhyming words that have the same vowel sound as the word in the box.

Follow-Up Activity

SUGGESTIONS:

RING	JAIL	GRAB	PAGE	REAL
thing	rail	jab	cage	meal
bring	pail	tab	wage	deal
ding	vail	slab	sage	steal
wing	flail	scab	guage	heal
ping	trail	nab	range	seal

BLAST	MAP	COAT	FIND	SHOWN
past	tap	goat	kind	thrown
fast	clap	moat	rind	blown
cast	lap	wrote	bind	flown
last	cap	note	grind	known
mast	gap	dote	hind	sown

Doing the Splits with Prefixes and Suffixes
Follow-Up Activity

1. vaulting
2. spotter
3. mats
4. dismount
5. approaching
6. pointer
7. practicing
8. recalled
9. tireless
10. extends, stretched
11. relive
12. reacted
13. disinterested
14. disappointed
15. dislike

Contract Skating

Many people don't believe how easy skating can really be. They make statements like "I don't know how to skate," "I can't do that," or "I'm too clumsy." But once they've learned how to skate, the "can'ts" seem to disappear. It's like learning to ride a bike, once you've learned how to skate; you'll never forget!

It takes practice to learn the basics of skating. Of course, there's a list of do's and don'ts to follow, but once you've mastered them you'll have no problems. Just remember that you're learning a new sport and it'll take time for you to become a pro. But if you'll take it one step at a time, it won't take you long to learn how to skate with great confidence.

An Old Sport

Silvio leads Tornado to 3–1 win

By Steve Tracy
Staff Writer of The News

Silvio's 2-goal performance spoiled Texas Tech product and Washington goalie Jim Messemer's NASL debut as Dallas handled the Diplomats, 3-1, at Texas Stadium Friday night.

The win is Dallas' third in four starts

■ **Tornado may move to different stadium. Page 2B**

after snapping a NASL record 20-game losing streak and the Tornado's second straight, but coach Peter Short pointed to a statistic more significant.

"This is the first time we have come from behind to win," said Short of the Tornado, down 1-0 at halftime. "This is something the team hasn't seen, which shows a new aggressiveness . . . an indication of a new spirit."

Silvio, the young leftwing from Brazil, scored his first two goals of the season. Both came in the second half against Messemer, who was making the first start of his professional career. He was replacing Jim Brown, who was sidelined with tendinitis. Messemer was the Dips' second-round draft pick after four years in goal for Texas Tech.

"The rookie (Messemer) played a great first half," Short said, "and handled some very difficult shots, but I think his inexperience showed in the second half, especially on Rausch's goal."

Off a pass from Silvio, right wing Wolfgang Rausch kicked one from 10-feet out that went right through Messemer's legs to tie the game, 1-1, at 67:05.

"It was an off-speed shot by Rausch," Short said, "and I think that really threw him off."

Three minutes later, Silvio booted in a 30-yarder past Messemer for his first score of the season, unassisted, with

69:57 gone for Dallas' first lead and then beat Washington defenders off a feed from Rausch at 88:04 for the final goal.

"Our first goal, while well engineered, was lucky," Short said "although Silvio's two goals were great. He's young . . . full of running.

"Our play tonight was more aggressive, which is what we are trying to achieve," Short said. "Our first half, we were a little anxious, but then in the second, we started attacking very well."

The Diplomats' loss was the third in a row for the team that is fighting for a NASL playoff berth.

"Injuries are hurting us . . . causing some major problems in our game," Washington coach Ken Furby said of the injured, now totaling half the team roster. "And we weren't aggressive tonight . . . the heat hurt to an extent with a good first half followed by a poor second."

Example of a suffix word (ance)	Example of a root word (fend)	Example of a compound word (some/thing)	Example of a word with both prefix (un) and suffix (ed)

	ROOT WORD	SUFFIX	PREFIX
a.	perform	ance	
b.	spoil	ed	
c.	lead	s	
d.	handle	ed	
e.	differ	ent	
f.	snap	ing	
g.	lose	ing	
h.	point	ed	
i.	aggress	ive, ness	
j.	indicate	tion	
k.	score	ed	
l.	tendon	itis	
m.	make	ing	
n.	profession	al	
o.	place	ing	re
p.	rook	ie	

	ROOT WORD	SUFFIX	PREFIX
q.	play	ed	
r.	special	ly	e
s.	real	ly	
t.	boot	ed	
u.	anxiety	ous	
v.	assist	ed	un

Follow-Up Activity

COMPOUND WORDS

1. play/off
2. off/speed
3. half/time
4. side/lined
5. some/thing
6. left/wing

Soccer Can Be Puzzling

ACROSS:

1. shoes
2. foul
3. kick
6. eleven

DOWN:

1. soccer
2. field
3. goal
5. team

Follow-Up Activity

forward—the player on the front line
goalie box—the area that is the goalie's responsibility
goalie—the player who defends the goal
fullback—the player who helps the goalie
circle—the place on the field where the game starts
throw-in—to put the ball into play from the sidelines
offside—not enough opponents between you and the goalie
passing—kicking the ball to a teammate

Soccer Suffixes
Follow-Up Activity

1. scored
2. trapped
3. dribbling
4. stop
5. kicking
6. yelled
7. pass
8. heading
9. centered
10. sprinting
11. lofted
12. block

Reading High Jumper
Follow-Up Activity

1. injury
2. event
3. lose
4. race
5. track
6. yard
7. sprint
8. stadium
9. baton
10. broad
11. ready
12. discuss
13. hurdles
14. spikes
15. throw
16. finish
17. speed
18. sweat
19. lead
20. distance

Middle School Activities

Believe It or Not

Sport: General

Purpose: To develop a student's ability to use reference materials to read and learn about the origins of unfamiliar sports; to develop a student's capacity to recall details and interpret diagrams.

Materials: Pencil

Discussion: One important school-related reading skill is reading to find specific information. Parents and teachers can use references of lesser-known sports to stimulate students to read, locate, and recall various facts. These may include interesting details related to play, equipment, dates, and places of origin, etc.

Directions: Below are several written accounts of some fairly uncommon sports in America. Read the brief description of each one and underline the specific facts or details related to these sports.

RUGBY

Rugby had its beginning at Rugby School in England in 1823. It is a sport similar to American football and soccer, in which 2 teams (with 13 players on a side) compete to score points by advancing the ball into the opponent's end zone or by kicking the ball through the goalposts. The grassy field is 110 yards long and 75 yards wide.

Rugby (called rugger in England) is a rough contact sport that demands superb conditioning and stamina. It is a game of running, passing (only lateral and backward tosses), kicking, and tackling but without any protective gear, substitutions, or time-outs. It has a continuous flow with rapid change of ball possession.

RUGBY PLAYING FIELD

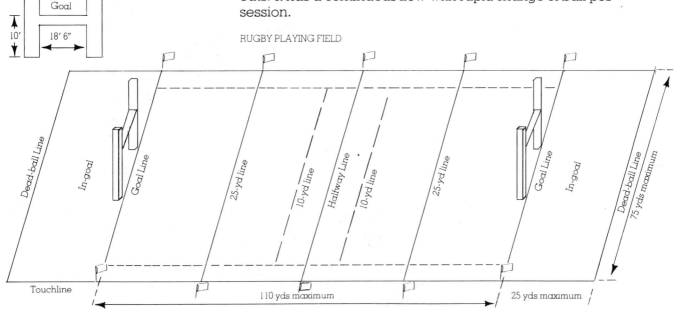

A typical and frequent event in a rugby match is the scrummage or set scrum, which results from a minor penalty called by the referee. Teammates hold each other in a 3-4-1 alignment and come together headfirst against the opposing pack. Once the ball is put in play, each group masses its combined strength against the other. At the same time, the players try to hook the ball backward with their feet and direct it to one of the backs, who then initiates an offensive action.

CRICKET

Cricket's origin is unknown. The name probably came from the Old English "cryce," meaning "stick," and in its crude form, resembled the 13th-century game known as club-ball. Modern cricket evolved in England in the 18th century, mainly because of the great landowners who tried their skills on a field of play with their tenants.

It is played with a bat and ball on a large field, known as a ground, between 2 teams of 11 players each. This centers upon 2 upright wickets, each defended by a batsman. A bowler (pitcher) bowls (a straight-arm, usually overhand, delivery) the ball, attempting to dismiss (put out) the batsman by hitting the wicket. Runs are scored each time the batsmen exchange positions without being dismissed.

PITCH AND POSITIONS

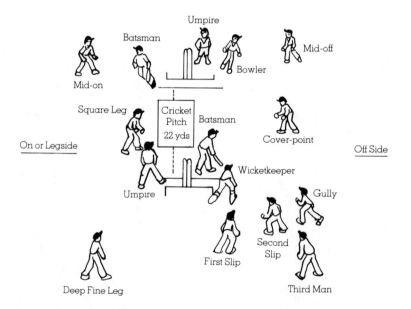

Each side has 2 innings, normally taken alternately. Matches are played for a predetermined amount of time, and often 2 days or more are necessary to finish.

The ground has no set dimensions. It may be circular or oval and must be limited to a maximum of 75 yards in any direction from its center.

The bat has a willow striking face (38″ long) and a cane handle layered with thin strips of rubber bound with the twine and covered with a sheath of rubber. The ball has a hand-stitched red leather cover and an interior of cork wound with twine. A cricketer's uniform is white: shirt, trousers, boots, and sweater.

LACROSSE

Lacrosse began as the Native American game, baggataway. It was played using a stick with a rawhide bag for throwing and catching the ball. This stick was similar to a bishop's crosier, so the early explorers renamed the Indian game lacrosse.

The crosse or stick, made of bent hickory with a triangle netting of catgut, is used for catching, carrying, and throwing the ball. The lacrosse ball is made of rubber and weighs around 5 ounces.

Lacrosse is played by 2 teams of 7 players each. The play is started from the center of the field by a face-off between the 2 center players.

Players are penalized for rule infractions by suspension from the game for a certain time. They leave the field and go to a penalty box.

The object of lacrosse is to send the ball through or into the rival's goal as many times as possible within the regulation period of play, which is 60 minutes. This is divided into 4 periods of 15 minutes each. A goal counts as one point.

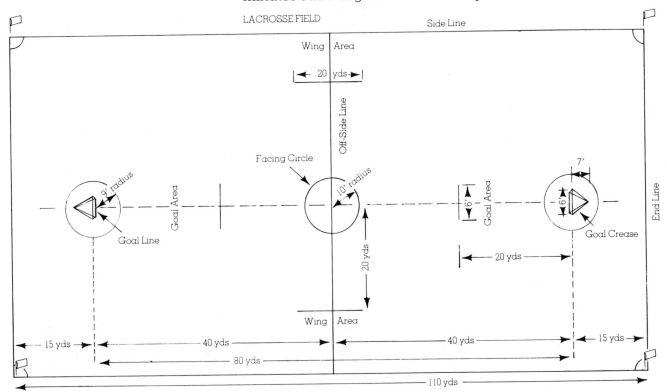

LACROSSE FIELD

LAWN TENNIS

Lawn tennis began in 1873, when a British army officer, Walter C. Wingfield, adapted the rules and techniques of court tennis to devise a game to be played on grass. The original court resembled an hourglass, measuring 60' in length, with 30' base lines and a 21' center line. The players played with a rubber ball and an oval-shaped racket. Two or 4 players played at a time on the court.

The next year, Wingfield patented his invention under the name of Sphairistike. He soon settled on the name "lawn tennis" because the former term was difficult to pronounce. Within a year, the hourglass shape was replaced by a rectangular shape with the present court dimensions (78' in length and 36' in width for doubles).

LAWN TENNIS COURT

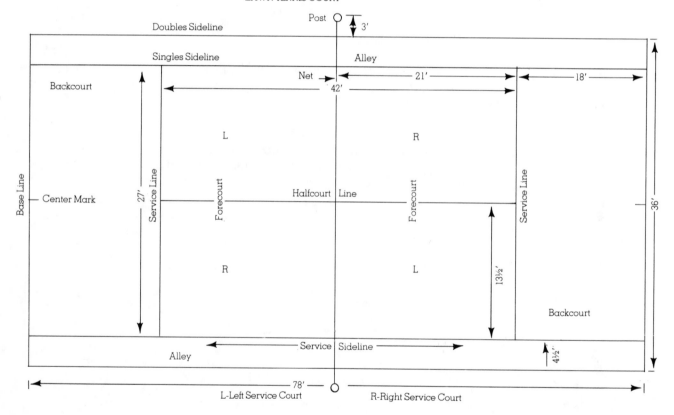

POLO

Polo began as early as the 1st century AD in Persia (now Iran). It is played on horseback between 2 teams of 4 players each who use mallets with long, flexible handles to drive a wooden ball down a grass field (300 yards in length by 200 yards in width) and between 2 goalposts.

A player's equipment usually consists of boots, white breeches, knee guards, whip, spurs, mallet, helmet, and a jersey. Polo ponies are not of any special breed or size. Thoroughbreds and three-quarter thoroughbreds are generally considered the most acceptable. It takes 6 months to a year to train a polo pony.

POLO FIELD

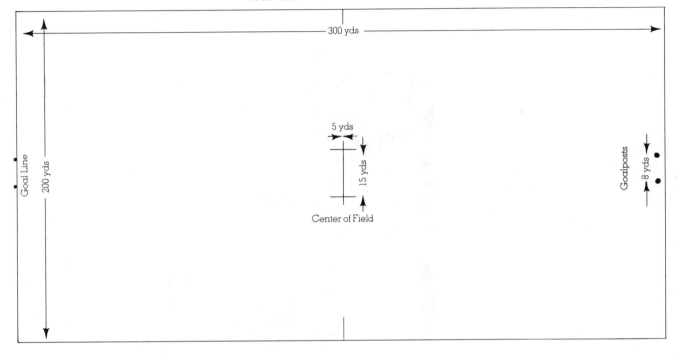

KORFBALL

Korfball, which resembles basketball, handball, and netball, was first played in 1902 in The Netherlands. The object of the game is to throw the ball so that it goes through the basket from above, scoring one point.

Korfball is played outdoors by 2 teams of 12 (6 women and 6 men) on a rectangular field of 100 yards in length and 45 yards in width. A short distance inside the end line (at either end of the field) is a goalpost supporting a cylindrical basket hoop. The rim of the basket is 11½' above the ground. The basket is 17" in diameter and the ball is about 8½" in diameter and weighs 14-16 ounces.

The field is divided into 3 zones, each occupied by 2 men and 2 women from each team. Their movement is confined to their zone. A game consists of 12 45-minute halves, and play begins with a free pass from center. Action consists almost entirely of passing the ball from hand to hand and from one zone to the next. Kicking, punching, handing off, running with the ball, and passing the ball over an intervening zone are illegal. Although no body contact is permitted, close guarding is done with opponents of the same sex. A penalty shot from a penalty mark 13' away is given to the victim of a major violation of the rules.

After 2 goals are made, players move to the next zone: defense to center, center to attack, and attack to defense. This places the players in a variety of playing positions.

KORFBALL

Have the student fill in blanks in the sentences below, incorporating facts that s/he has gathered from the preceeding descriptions.

rugby   lacrosse   polo
cricket   lawn tennis   korfball

1. _____ is for 2 or 4 players.

    ⬚⬚⬚⬚⬚   ⬚⬚⬚⬚⬚⬚
                         2   1

2. _____ began in 1823.

   5

3. _____ is related to handball, basketball, and netball.

   3

4. The object of _____ is to score by catching, carrying, or throwing the ball toward or into the opponent's goal.

   4

5. In _____, players are mounted on horses with long sticks to hit a wooden ball.

6. _____ is played on a large field centering upon 2 wickets each defended by a batsman.

   8

7. _____ involves handling, kicking, and dribbling the ball. Lateral passing, tackling, and the scrum are some aspects the game.

8. _____ evolved in 1873 in England.

   6

   7   10

9. _____ is of Dutch origin and began in 1902.

   9

10. _____ is played with a ball and a stick with a net on one end. There are 10 players on a team.

Have the student write the letters from the numbered boxes on the numbered spaces below to form a word that represents details and facts.

_____ _____ _____ _____ _____   𝓂   _____ _____ _____ _____ _____
 1   2   3   4   5   6   7   8   9   10

Answers, page 155

Follow-Up Activity: Ask the student to select one of the sports in this activity that s/he would like to know more about. Provide him/her with an encyclopedia to locate additional information. Then ask the student to write a letter describing this sport to a friend. After this is done, go over the letter with the student and underline all the details s/he was able to cite in reference to this game.

Dear _____:

_____

_____

_____

_____

_____

_____

_____

_____

_____

It's All in the Name

Sport: General

Purpose: To develop a student's fluent word-recognition and oral-reading skills.

Materials: Pencil, paper, list of nicknames

Discussion: Parents and teachers can use sports-team names to develop tongue-twister word-recognition reading and writing activities. These challenge a student to recognize words in print that have the same or similar spelling patterns and sounds. The student must pronounce each word correctly and concentrate on reading smoothly.

Directions: Read and discuss with the student the following examples of sports team tongue twisters:

---

1. Several successive goals were scored by the San Diego Sockers.
2. The Cleveland Cavaliers clearly came close to clubbing the clowns from Connersville.
3. The Seattle Seahawks saved the game by scoring 7 goals.

Then direct the student to use the following list of team nicknames to write sentences containing tongue twisters:

LIST OF TEAM NICKNAMES:

HOCKEY

Philadelphia Flyers
Pittsburgh Penguins
Boston Bruins

BASKETBALL

New York Knicks
New Jersey Nets
Los Angeles Lakers
Seattle Supersonics
San Antonio Spurs

SOCCER

Seattle Sounders
Los Angeles Aztecs
Philadelphia Fury
Houston Hurricane

BASEBALL

Philadelphia Phillies
Pittsburgh Pirates
Chicago Cubs
New York Yankees

FOOTBALL

Buffalo Bills
Tampa Bay Buccaneers
Kansas City Chiefs
San Francisco 49ers

Follow-Up Activity: Present the following athletes' names to the student and ask him/her to write a paragraph incorporating numerous tongue twisters. To develop reading fluency, these brief stories may be read orally to the parent or teacher.

MOSES MALONE

Moses Malone managed to make many points during the Memorial Day game. Moses most likely matched his skill that day with many of the best players in the basketball world. Malone might become a major sports hero in the marvelous world of "My Main Man" basketball.

POSSIBLE NAMES TO USE:

1. Alexis Arguello (boxing)

2. Gayle Goodrich (basketball)

3. Sam Snead (golf)

4. Bobby Bonds (baseball)

5. Bjorn Borg (tennis)

6. Mike McEwen (hockey)

7. John Jefferson (football)

Pass the Sports Word

Sport: General

Purpose: To improve a student's ability to concentrate; to strengthen word-recognition skills.

Materials: List of passwords, paper, pencil, stopwatch

Discussion: Parents and teachers can use the format of the television game show "Password" in the context of sports to enhance a student's ability to concentrate and to reinforce word-recognition skills. By using familiar sports terms for the passwords, parents and teachers can make the game one of high interest for many students.

Directions: The following game is played like "Password" but requires only 2 players. Before beginning play, make sure each student has a "Sports Passwords" list, located at the end of this activity. The object of the game is for one player to provide the other player a clue word that allows him/her to guess a particular sports password. Each player has 10 seconds to guess the word. If a player guesses correctly on the first clue word, s/he receives 10 points. If a player guesses a form of the password, s/he gets one chance to self-correct and say the exact password. A total of 10 clue words may be given for each password. The point value diminishes by one with each clue word given. If a player needs 5 clue words to guess a password, s/he would only receive 5 points. After both players have gone through their list of passwords, the score is totaled and the player with the most points wins. See example below.

> Player 1 selects the first password from his/her list. The word is <u>team</u>. Without revealing this word to the other person, s/he provides a clue word. An example would be <u>group</u>.
>
> Player 2 tries to guess the password from the clue-word group. If Player 2 guesses correctly on the first clue word, s/he would receive 10 points.

The following are rules that should be used with the clue words:

- The clue word must be a single, nonhyphenated word.
- Proper persons, places, or things may be used as clue words.
- The clue word cannot contain any part or form of the password.
- A player can repeat a clue word if s/he deems it necessary.
- A player cannot spell a clue word.

"A" List of Sports Passwords	"B" List of Sports Passwords
1. halftime	1. team
2. World Series	2. home run
3. league	3. score
4. game	4. puck
5. champion	5. kick
6. diamond	6. player
7. rebound	7. corner
8. period	8. football
9. bout	9. pitcher
10. field goal	10. basketball
11. dribble	11. goalie
12. base	12. point
13. steal	13. serve
14. Super Bowl	14. knock-out
15. fight	15. touchdown
16. opponent	16. field
17. coach	17. court
18. dugout	18. arena
19. safety	19. victory
20. net	20. racket
21. singles	21. punch
22. heavyweight	22. stadium
23. titleholder	23. dunking
24. defeat	24. penalty
25. manager	25. goal

Follow-Up Activity: Ask the students to prepare their own lists of 25 passwords using terms from their favorite sport. Have the students work in pairs to prepare the list of passwords and then play as partners during the game. Team A can compete against Team B and the team that can accumulate the most points wins the game.

Reading Between or Beyond the Lines

Sport: General

Purpose: To improve a student's understanding of figurative language, which is often used in composing the headlines of sports articles; to enhance a student's use of figurative expressions in his/her own writing.

Materials: Assortment of headlines cut from sports articles in newspapers or magazines, scissors, glue, large sheet of paper (such as manila paper), pencil or pen

Discussion: Frequently, the fluent speaker of a language is a person who has a strong grasp of figurative expressions. Using sports magazines and newspaper sports sections, clip story headlines which have utilized figurative language such as the following:

"NFC Central: Sims steals the spotlight"
"Fans up in arms over ticket prices"
"Baseball season put on hold after Thursday?"

The underlined words in the above headlines have been used in a figurative way by the authors. In reading these headlines, one must look beyond the literal meaning of these words. Sports-writers often employ this technique to make their articles eye-catching.

DID YOU SAY,
"The Fans Are Up in Arms?"

Directions: Cut out headlines from sports articles in the newspaper that contain figurative terms or expressions. Glue each headline next to the left margin on a blank sheet of paper. Leave several inches between each headline. Divide the rest of the page into 2 equally wide columns. Label one column "literal meaning" and the other "student's interpretation." See the following example. Have the student read each headline carefully and discuss the literal meaning of it. Next, discuss what the headline may mean or its figurative meaning. Make certain that the student records both the literal and figurative definitions as a means for comparison.

HEADLINES	LITERAL MEANING	STUDENT'S INTERPRETATION
"Retama buries Fort Worth club to capture title"		*A team named Retama beat a Fort Worth team to win a Championship.*

"Battle for NFC East title seen as strictly a 2-team race"

"All washed up?"

"Cards whip Phils to snap losing streak"

"Rogers rides herd at Western Open"

"Can wilting Twins flower under the Gardner's care?"

"Australia next up in Cup"

"Home run king Creel emerges from brother's shadow"

"Tornado gets stung again for 20th loss"

Follow-Up Activity: Provide articles for a student to read with the headlines missing. Ask the student to read each story and write a good, figurative headline for the article. Following is an example of one article that lends itself to this type of activity.

> Jockey Larry Saumell, one of New York's most successful riders, has been barred from Aqueduct, Belmont and Saratoga racetracks pending results of a New York Racing Association investigation. Saumell has been accused of using an illegal battery device to stimulate one of his mounts last June 22. Saumell could lose his jockey's license if he fails to cooperate with the investigation or is found guilty. In a reversal for Saumell, racing officials are applying the whip to the jockey.

From Wire Reports

Afterwards, discuss the student's choice of figurative language and the use of each expression in his/her headline. Appropriate headlines for the above article might include:

"Illegal Use of Battery Gets Jockey Charged"
"Racing Officials Apply Whip to Jockey"
"Jockey Thrown from Races Pending Investigation"

The actual headline for the above article read:
"Barred Jockey Faces Possible License Loss"
The by-line read: "Power to Spare."

Sports Detective

Sport: General

Purpose: To develop a student's comprehension skills through an understanding of numerous multiple-meaning expressions; to develop an ability to use context—the parts of a sentence immediately next to or surrounding a specified word that determine its exact meaning.

Materials: Pencil

Discussion: Many words in our language have multiple meanings. These words must be understood in their specific context if a reader is to grasp an author's meaning. For example, the word "dribble" may have several meanings. The following sentences demonstrate 2 meanings of the word "dribble."

It's not a big leak under the sink; it's just a <u>dribble</u>—meaning: a flowing in small drops.

<u>Dribble</u> the ball to the goal—meaning: to keep a ball in motion or move it forward by a rapid succession of bounces.

Various sports employ a wide range of multiple-meaning expressions. Becoming acquainted with these terms adds a great deal of understanding and interest to the games and events themselves.

Parents or teachers can help a student become acquainted with multiple-meaning words by providing him/her with sentences such as those presented in this activity. These contain a large store of multiple-meaning terms.

Directions: Have the student read each pair of sentences and determine the word that fits into each one. Use the sentence below as an example.

A long, heavy nail used to build railroads is called a *spike*.

For a *spike*, the player leaps at the net and smashes the ball with his/her hand into the opponent's court.

---

1.   When one of the tires went flat, she used the _____ from the trunk.

He made a _____ by knocking over all 10 pins with 2 consecutive rolls of the ball.

2. He was sent to jail after he was caught _____ things that did not belong to him.

   In _____ a base, it's important to watch the pitcher's eyes so you won't be thrown out.

3. They planned to _____ the beef and rice with a salad.

   He won the point with a speedy slice _____ to the opponent's side of the court.

4. There was excitement at the rodeo arena as the cowboys gathered at the _____ .

   The pitcher was warming up in the _____.

5. The magician performed a _____ _____ for the children and pulled a bunny out.

   A _____ _____ is when a single player propels the puck across the opponent's goal 3 times in one game.

6. The 2 book _____ met together to plan the special program.

   Wood _____ are longer than iron _____. A player usually carries 4 woods and 10 irons.

7. The workers decided to _____ for higher wages.

   The third _____ puts the batter out.

8. Do you want a _____, _____, or _____ dip of ice cream?

   A _____ is a hit enabling a batter to reach first base; a _____ is a hit enabling a batter to reach second base; a _____ is a hit enabling a batter to reach third base.

9. The nurse gave the child a _____ in the arm to help him get well.

   A one-handed jump _____ is effective in a crowded area or for a free-throw _____ .

10. The recipe called for a _____ of salt.

    The _____ hitter came through with a score for the team.

11. The movie was about a beautiful _____ story in which the couple lived happily forever.

    The backhand stroke made the score _____ –30. With this game he would win the match.

12. The bus only made a _____ _____ in each small town.

The _____ plays between second and third base.

13. The _____ was filled with delicious-looking chicken.

The catcher dusted off home _____.

14. The dish had been dropped and had a _____ out of it.

A shot made from just off the green is called a _____ shot.

15. She held the _____ to her ear as she talked on the telephone.

The wide _____ caught the pass.

16. A Saturday chore was to wash and _____.

_____ clubs are identified by numbers one–9.

Answers, page 155

Follow-Up Activity: From each pair of sentences in the preceding activity, have the student reread the sentence that pertains to sports. Ask the student to note words in the sentence which give the reader a clue about the name of the sport which regularly uses the term. In the following manner, the student should write the clue words from the sentence, then write the name of the sport as determined from these clues. Being a good detective means uncovering as many of these words as possible.

CLUE WORDS	NAME OF SPORT
leaps, net, hand, court	*volleyball*

After the student has completed the above activity, discuss the clue words taken from the sentences as they refer to a particular sport. Compare the student's conclusions with those on the parent's or teacher's page. Children may enjoy searching through sports articles for more multiple-meaning words used in various sports. The students may be encouraged to write their own sentence pairs to demonstrate the multiple meanings of the words they discover.

Answers, page 155

Try My Way!

Sport: General

Purpose: To develop a student's higher-level comprehension skills of sequencing, analyzing, comparing, or making inferences; to encourage creative writing.

Materials: Original sports cartoon sketch or newspaper comic strip, plain paper which is as large as the comic strip, pencil, glue, scissors, stapler

Discussion: A student's continued growth in reading is dependent upon his/her ability to recognize sequence, analyze information, compare and contrast ideas, and make inferences about materials they have read. These higher-level comprehension skills may be highlighted in the following creative writing activities.

Directions: The parent or teacher should cut speech bubbles from any sports-related cartoon. Staple the cartoon frames onto a background of plain paper. Glue the author's original speech bubbles onto another sheet of paper in their correct sequence.

Reprinted by permission: © 1961 United Feature Syndicate Inc.

Give the student the sports cartoon portion with speech bubbles removed. (Since the cartoon has been placed over a sheet of plain paper, the student will have a place to write.) Ask the student to write in what s/he thinks the characters are saying in each frame. Then, ask him/her to read each of the author's original "speech bubbles." Enjoy comparing the student's version and the original. This may also be done as a group activity.

Follow-Up Activity:

To teach sequencing, cut out another sports-related cartoon frame by frame. Number the back of each frame to correspond to the original sequence.

Jumble the order of these frames and spread them out on a table in front of the student. Ask the student to put them into the correct story order. When s/he has finished, turn the frames over and compare the author's original story sequence with that of the student. Discuss similarities and differences. When the student's version varies from the author's, ask him/her to explain why s/he thought a particular frame seemed to fit in that position. If his/her answer is justifiable or logical, there is no need to change the sequence. If, on the other hand, the sequence is obviously illogical, help the student understand why an alternative frame would be more appropriate.

Who Says So?

Sport: General

Purpose: To develop a student's critical reading skills by teaching him/her to read and evaluate the sometimes duplicitous language of advertising.

Materials: Paper, pencils, synopses of ads with sports figures endorsing products

Discussion: Advertisers have long used sports personalities in ad campaigns to endorse all types of products. Many students especially, can be swayed by these ads because they fail to read critically. They identify the product with a person who they may regard as a role model. Students can be taught to read critically and analyze advertising testimonials by pinpointing advertising methods and questioning their purposes.

For example, a tire company ad pictures Roger Staubach and states, "Roger Staubach—one of the most dependable performers in football history: and an engineer by training." It goes on to say that this tire has "performance built-in" and a "longer tread life."

The implications are that (a) Roger Staubach uses these tires on his own car, (b) the tires are dependable and good performers like Roger, and (c) since Roger was trained as an engineer, he is technically qualified to evaluate tires. These ideas are misleading because (a) it doesn't say that Roger uses the tires, (b) Roger's dependability and performance have nothing to do with the quality of a tire, and (c) being an engineer does not qualify Roger as a tire expert.

Directions: Begin a discussion of product endorsements by asking the student to name commercials s/he has viewed which show sports figures recommending products. Using these and the preceeding Roger Staubach example, ask the student to answer the following questions:

1. What sports personality is endorsing this product?

2. Does the product relate in any way to the endorser's sport or area of expertise?

3. Why do you think this particular person was chosen for this ad?

4. What qualities does s/he have that the company wants you to associate with their product?

5.   What implications does the ad make? Are these implications misleading? Why or why not?

6.   What catchy phrases are used to grab your attention?

Have the student read the following excerpts of magazine advertisements. Then have him/her write the answers to the preceeding questions and discuss them.

Ad #1   An ad for a book which teaches children to play tennis has a picture of several small kids holding rackets almost as big as they are. The headline reads, "Did Tracy Austin start this way?" and goes on to say that yes, as a matter of fact, she did, and that the author of this book taught her to play tennis.

Ad #2   An ad for a brand of golf balls reads, "Golf's 2 most durable performers are both named Hogan."

Ad #3   An ad for a brand of watches pictures Arnold Palmer in midswing and reads:
It's more than the private jets, the lucrative entrepreneurial ventures, and the television commentary. It's style. The Palmer style . . . he's reinforced his reputation every step of the way. Like the watch he wears . . . a testament to style, to endurance, to timeless value.

Ad #4   An ad for an investment firm uses Tom Watson to tell us that by listening to this company's advice one can learn how to "stay ahead of that inflation bogey."

Ad #5   A headline for a sportswear ad introduces "The Newest Doubles Team in Tennis. . . . "Harold Soloman and this line of tennis wear. It asks you to let this product make you a winner on and off the courts.

Ad #6   A grinning Walt Garrison holds up a snuff can (Super Bowl ring clearly in view). The ad reads, "Go smokeless. It's the only way to go."

Ad #7   Lee Trevino, driver in hand, points to a steel-belted radial tire and says, "I'm not the first to tell you that the grip is important when you drive." The ad continues, "Freeway or fairway, on the roads or in the rough, grip is important."

Follow-Up Activity: Have the student search newspapers and magazines to find at least 5 ads which contain sports personality testimonials. Ask him/her to analyze the ads using questions from the previous activity. Then have the student create an ad for a product using a current sports hero's imaginary testimony to endorse it.

Wide World of Cause and Effect

Sport: General

Purpose: To improve comprehension by encouraging a student to recognize and use cause-and-effect relationships; to expand a student's vocabulary by introducing specific terms related to various sports.

Materials: Paper, pencil, list of cause-and-effect statements

Discussion: Much of what a student must read requires him/her to recognize cause-and-effect relationships. A cause is something that occasions a result and an effect is a condition or occurrence directly traceable to the cause. Each student can improve his/her comprehension by learning to identify, understand, and use these relationships. To help a student make a clear distinction between cause and effect, introduce him/her to the following example:

> 1. John put his hand on the hot stove.
> 2. John burned his hand badly.

The fact that John put his hand on the hot stove is the cause. The effect of John putting his hand on the stove is that he burned his hand. Number 2 happened because of number one.

To make sure the student understands this concept, ask him/her to identify the cause and the effect in the following statement:

> Susan forgot to set the alarm and was late for the game.
>
> (cause) Because _____,
> (effect) Susan was _____.

Directions: Have the student match the effect in column 2 with the appropriate situation in column 1. Before beginning the exercise, have the student scan the underlined words in column 1. Explain the sports-related context of each set of words.

1	2
A. John McEnroe throws a temper tantrum on the court at <u>Wimbledon</u> and yells at a <u>line judge</u>.	1. The coach was <u>fired</u>.
B. The race car driver entered the <u>curve too quickly</u>.	2. The boat <u>capsized</u>.
C. The golfer <u>hooked</u> his <u>drive</u>.	3. The football team was <u>penalized</u> 5 yards.
D. The tackle jumped <u>offside</u>.	4. The great tennis star is <u>fined</u> $10,000.
E. The offensive linemen <u>failed</u> to <u>block</u>.	5. The skier was <u>disqualified</u> from the race.
F. The team <u>did</u> <u>not</u> <u>win</u> a game all season.	6. It was a <u>false start</u> and the runners had to line up at the starting line again.
G. The tennis player scored an <u>ace</u> on his first serve of the game.	7. The car <u>spun</u> <u>out</u> of <u>control</u> and smashed into the wall.
H. One runner <u>jumped</u> <u>the gun</u>.	8. The ball landed in the <u>rough</u>.
I. The <u>mainsail</u> fell.	9. The quarterback was <u>trapped</u>.
J. The <u>slalom</u> <u>racer</u> missed a gate.	10. The score was 15-<u>love</u>.

Answers, page 155

Follow-Up Activity: Write a possible cause for each of these effects:

1. The cowboy received no score in the bullriding event.
possible cause: _____

_____

2. The hockey player was put in the penalty box.
possible cause: _____

_____

3. The manager was thrown out of the game.
possible cause: _____

_____

4. The golf ball landed in the sand trap.
possible cause: _____

_____

5. The gymnast fell off the balance beam.
possible cause: _____

_____

6. The boxing match lasted only 2 of the scheduled 10 rounds.
   possible cause: _____

   _____

7. The batter was awarded a ground-rule double.
   possible cause: _____

   _____

8. The glass backboard was shattered by the force of "Chocolate Thunder's" dunk.
   possible cause: _____

   _____

9. Dr. J was awarded 2 free throws.
   possible cause: _____

   _____

10. The center fielder dropped the routine pop fly.
    possible cause: _____

    _____

The Hard Charger and the Bridesmaid

Sport: Auto Racing

Purpose: To develop a student's literal and inferential comprehension skills by introducing questions that are related to a newspaper sports article on automobile racing.

Materials: Paper, pencils

Discussion: To understand everything we read is a difficult task. Comprehension is a learned skill and as such requires much practice. Anatole France (1844–1924), a famous French writer and literary critic, once said, "It is better to understand little than to misunderstand much." Parents and teachers can make good use of sports-related newspaper and magazine articles to teach students that an author's meaning may be stated literally (upholding the concrete interpretation of a word, sentence, passage, or selection) or inferentially (to draw a conclusion or make a deduction based on facts that are not specifically stated but must be assumed or induced). Frequently students read not only for factual understanding but must use the facts or specific information to infer an author's meaning. This means they must not only "read the lines" but must be able to "read between and beyond" them.

Directions: Ask the student to read the sports article on the following page and underline 5 specifically stated facts, for example:

> In the second paragraph, the fact that Yarborough won the race is specifically stated.

After reading the article and underlining these pieces of information, direct the student to read the following 5 paragraphs taken from the news story and answer the accompanying questions by circling the letter next to the best answer.

Cagey Yarborough wins Firecracker

By Gary Long
Knight-Ridder Wire

DAYTONA BEACH, Fla.—Cale Yarborough, hardest of the hard chargers, found himself a "gentleman race driver" Saturday and took advantage of him.

Yarborough rode the back bumper of Harry Gant's Buick most of the last 50 miles and then whipped past on the inside just one mile from the finish to win Daytona's Firecracker 400 for the fourth time.

Never a winner on the NASCAR Grand National circuit, Gant became a bridesmaid for the eighth time in the last year and a half. Nice guys finish second; but they finish.

Yarborough fully expected Gant to leave him racing room when he made his inside move at the end of the back straightway on this 2¼-mile trioval. "I know Harry Gant was the type man I didn't have to worry about," he said, meaning it as a compliment.

And what if Gant had eased down a couple grooves to try to pinch him against the infield grass? "Were you here in '79?" Yarborough responded.

The reference was to the 1979 Daytona 500. Yarborough tried the same slingshot move on Donnie Allison, again entering the third turn, again on the last lap, and Allison refused to yield.

They proceeded to bang together three times before crashing into the wall, and they ended up fighting in the third-turn infield grass while Richard Petty celebrated a gift victory.

Oddly, Petty's Buick was nipping at the heels of the frontrunners, with Buddy Baker just a few car-lengths further back, but they settled for third and fourth as Yarborough beat Gant to the line by a car-length.

"I knew if I could get into the third turn going flat-out and keep my momentum that there was no way he (Gant) could beat me back to the line," Yarborough said.

Gant, at 41 the same age as Yarborough but a relative latecomer to Grand National racing, took defeat philosophically, "There was nothing I could do to hold him off," he said. "I had tried to zig-zag across the race track to keep him from getting around me, but obviously it didn't work."

A crowd estimated at 65,000 on another of those hazy, crazy Daytona days of summer still experienced plenty of thrills without a last-lap crash for a capper.

The yellow flag flew on six occasions, slowing the field for 37 of the 160 laps, for blown engines, three single car mishaps and a wild and terrifying six-car tangle.

Yarborough, who banked $24,675 to Gant's $15,350 from a purse exceeding $260,000, appeared to have the edge in his M.C. Anderson-owned Buick. Though there were 35 official lead changes among 10 drivers, Yarborough led 78 laps.

"We've got a new set of circumstances down here," said Neil Bonnett, whose run of hard luck this season continued when the engine on his Wood Brothers Ford blew after 93 hard laps.

"The new cars (mid-sized models mandated by NASCAR this season) are really squirrelly when they're running together. If one car can break away, like Cale did, he can hold it wide open through the turns. But the guys in the pack have to back off because the cars are scooting and jumping around.

In fact, Yarborough was able to run away and leave the field in his wake twice. But after the final caution period, during which Yarborough took on four new tires, he seemed to have lost part of his advantage.

"The race track got a little greasier and my car got a little looser," he said. "I was afraid to try to break away again. You've got to use your head a little bit in this race business. It took patience, and it's hard to be patient for 30 laps. But I knew what I had to do and did it.

He and Gant swapped the lead back and forth twice. But that, Yarborough said, was just "testing" of Gant. He said, "He will win. He's got a good team."

The caution periods slowed Yarborough's average speed to 142.588 mph, a far cry from the record 173.473 winning run of Bobby Allison in the 1980 Firecracker. Allison, a four-time winner and the Grand National points leader this year, was trying to chase down Yarborough near the 275-mile mark when his engine quit.

The victory was Yarborough's 71st in an illustrious career, his second in nine 1981 events in his trimmed-back schedule.

Dallas Times Herald, July 5, 1981
Answers, page 156

Editor's Note: On April 25, 1982 Harry Gant won the Virginia 500 capturing his first NASCAR victory.

1. Yarborough fully expected Gant to leave him racing room when he made his inside move at the end of the back straightway on his 2¼-mile trioval. "I know Harry Gant was the type man I didn't have to worry about," he said, meaning it as a compliment.

Why did Yarborough expect Gant to leave him some racing room when he made his move?
a) Yarborough knew his driving ability was better than Gant's.
b) Gant was always known to be a strictly second place finisher.
c) Yarborough knew of Gant's reputation of being a "gentle-man race driver."

2. The yellow flag flew on 6 occasions, slowing the field for 37 of the 160 laps, for blown engines, 3 single-car mishaps, and a wild and terrifying 6-car tangle.

The yellow flag was flown for 37 of the 160 total laps, which implies that almost _____ of the race was run under a caution flag.
a) 25%
b) 18%
c) 30%

3. "The new cars (mid-sized models mandated by NASCAR this season) are really squirrelly when they're running together. If one car can break away, like Cale did, he can hold it wide open through the turns. But the guys in the pack have to back off because the cars are scooting and jumping around."

The new mid-sized cars:
a) are easier to handle than the previous full-size cars.
b) are required by NASCAR rules.
c) perform well on any type of track surface.

4. Gant, at 41 the same age as Yarborough but a relative latecomer to Grand National racing, took defeat philosophically, "There was nothing I could do to hold him off," he said. "I had tried to zig-zag across the race track to keep him from getting around me, but obviously it didn't work."

Using context clues, what do you think the author means in the phrase, "took defeat philosophically?"

a) Gant had a noncaring attitude.
b) Gant was satisfied he had finished the race according to his own set of values.
c) Gant was admitting that Yarborough was a better driver.

5. In fact, Yarborough was able to run away and leave the field in his wake twice. But after the final caution period, during which Yarborough took on 4 new tires, he seemed to have lost part of his advantage.

Why did Yarborough lose part of his advantage?
a) His car developed engine trouble.
b) The new tires overheated easily, causing him to slow down.
c) The new tires were not suited to the track conditions.

To reinforce the student's ability to recognize facts and make inferences, ask him/her to answer the following questions either true or false, based on the previous sports article.

Answers, page 156

Follow-Up Activity:

1. _____ Yarborough led the race for 78 laps, which was over half of the race.

2. _____ The difference in the amount of money won between first and second place was $9,325.00

3. _____ Yarborough's character is described by a word in the title of the article.

4. _____ Gant had finished in second place 4 times in the last year-and-a-half.

5. _____ Yarborough's victory was his ninth in 1981.

6. _____ "Squirrelly" means to scoot and jump around.

7. _____ Neil Bonnett's engine blew up after completion of three-fourths of the race.

8. _____ Yarborough received approximately one-tenth of the total prize money for first place.

9. _____ Gant and Yarborough both drove Buicks.

10. _____ Buddy Baker and Richard Petty placed fifth and sixth in the race.

Answers, page 156

Crossword Puzzle—American League Teams

Sport: Baseball

Purpose: To develop a student's spelling and word recognition skills; to provide an academic context in which to apply his/her knowledge of baseball.

Materials: Pencil

Discussion: Crossword puzzles can be used to motivate students to practice reading and writing skills. Since many students have a high degree of interest in sports, these puzzles can be developed using sports information as the content. This provides students many opportunities to practice spelling an assortment of vocabulary items and drawing conclusions based on the clues.

Directions: Have the student complete the following crossword puzzle with the names of American League baseball teams.

ACROSS

1. Enemies of the cowboys in western movies
5. In the Civil War, the Rebels (South) fought the _____ (North).
6. Powerful, strong orange and black animals; members of cat family
7. Men such as fishermen who spend their lives at sea
12. Birds that are black and orange
13. When I play basketball, I always wear tennis shoes and _____ _____ on my feet.
14. Three friends, Al, Roy, and Al combined their names to form the name of the team called _____.

DOWN

2. Outlaw motorcycle gang, the Hell's _____
3. More than one masked man, "The Lone _____"
4. All alphabets begin with _____ (plural).
8. Scarlet feet coverings
9. Makers of beer
10. Larry and Moe are brothers who look almost exactly alike. They are _____.
11. Birds that are colored blue

Answers, page 156

Follow-Up Activity: Match the names of the American League baseball teams in the second column with the correct city and/or state in the first:

CITY/STATE	TEAM
_____ A. New York	1. Rangers
_____ B. Seattle	2. Twins
_____ C. Oakland	3. White Sox
_____ D. Cleveland	4. Yankees
_____ E. Texas	5. Blue Jays
_____ F. Chicago	6. Angels
_____ G. California	7. Red Sox
_____ H. Boston	8. Brewers
_____ I. Toronto	9. Mariners
_____ J. Baltimore	10. Orioles
_____ K. Kansas City	11. Indians
_____ L. Milwaukee	12. Tigers
_____ M. Minnesota	13. Royals
_____ N. Detroit	14. A's

Answers, page 156

It's a Steal

Sport: Baseball

Purpose: To build a student's vocabulary by using terms related to baseball.

Materials: Crossword puzzle, clues, pencils

Discussion: Providing a student with sports-related exercises may tap a rich reservoir of experience. Cultivating these experiences will develop his/her problem-solving skills and introduce the student to meaningful reading and writing activities. This approach encourages students not only to use what they already know in order to answer questions, but to apply the known to the unknown in an effort to furnish appropriate responses.

Directions: Present the crossword puzzle and clues on the following pages and have the student complete the crossword puzzle.

CLUES:

ACROSS

2. Scored when a player advances around the bases and touches home plate without being put out
3. Runs scored by a batter's hits, when s/he receives a base on balls, or when s/he is hit by a pitched ball
5. Any batted ball in fair territory which is not caught in mid-air or thrown to first base to get the batter out
7. A base runner runs safely from one base to another
9. Two teams playing 2 consecutive games
10. Batter taps the ball with his/her bat
11. A 3 base hit
12. Batter needs to bunt so runner can score from third base
14. Batter goes to first base after pitcher throws 4 balls while s/he is at bat
15. An area where players can warm up
16. Any pitch that crosses over the plate between the batter's shoulders and his/her knees
17. Any batted ball that lands ouside the foul lines

DOWN

1. Any batted ball that lands inside the foul lines
4. Percentage of times that a player gets a hit
6. This occurs when a runner on first base runs toward second as the pitcher pitches
8. Illegal act by a pitcher with one or more runners on base

12. Three strikes count as an out
13. When a batter intentionally bunts a ball and is put out so another runner can advance
15. Pitch at which the batter does not swing and does not cross over the plate in the correct location
18. Average number of runs a pitcher allows his opponents to score per 9 innings (abbreviation)

Answers, page 157

Follow-Up Activity: Ask the student to list 10 more baseball terms that were not included in this puzzle. An almanac is a good resource for this activity.

1. _____

2. _____

3. _____

4. _____

5. _____

6. _____

7. _____

8. _____

9. _____

10. _____

On with a Double (Meaning)

Sport: Baseball

Purpose: To expand understanding of multiple-meaning words by using them in different contexts.

Materials: Paper, pencil, sentences using multiple-meaning words in the context of baseball

Discussion: Many words have different meanings when used in a specific context. For example, a cell may refer to locked rooms that hold prisoners in jail or in a biological context, a cell refers to a microscopic mass of protoplasm. Students frequently encounter multiple-meaning vocabulary in their content area reading assignments. The ability to recognize different meanings for the same word in varying contexts is important to a student's higher-level reading comprehension.

Directions: Have the student develop sentences using the terms underlined below in the context of baseball. Have him/her write them in the blanks that follow.

Example: The bat flew out of the cave.

The ballplayer practiced swinging the bat.

---

1. Strike a match so we can see in here. _____
   _____

2. The fans are keeping the air cool. _____
   _____

3. Terrorists bombed the army base. _____
   _____

4. He was dipping a doughnut in his coffee. _____
   _____

5. Can you force him to do it? _____
   _____

6. Some people refer to marijuana as "grass." _____
   _____

7. Don't squeeze the Charmin! _____
   _____

8. Maybe this will jog your memory. _____
   _____

9. The young man is in the major part of his career. _____
   _____

10. Pour the tea from the pitcher. _____
    _____

11. What do you base your theory on? _____
    _____

12. The teacher told us to line up at the door. _____
    _____

13. Get the swatter so I can kill that fly. _____
    _____

14. I tipped the waiter $2. _____
    _____

15. Some pepper will make the stew taste better. _____
    _____

Follow-Up Activity: Match a definition of the underlined baseball-related term on the right to a sentence on the left that contains a word with that meaning used in a different context.

____ A. He's <u>out</u> of film.

____ B. She's the kind of person who <u>steals</u> the show.

____ C. There is a <u>foul</u> odor in here.

____ D. Mom <u>designated</u> me to do the cooking.

____ E. Indians made <u>dugouts</u>, or boats, by hollowing out logs.

____ F. The children <u>swing</u> for fun!

____ G. He will <u>balk</u> when asked to take out the garbage.

____ H. Your <u>shoestring</u> is loose.

____ I. The people who work in laundries, whitening clothes, are called <u>bleachers</u>.

____ J. The pot is on the back <u>burner</u>.

____ K. Mom poured the cake <u>batter</u> into the pan.

____ L. I have a <u>mound</u> of homework to do.

____ M. The train conductor yelled, "All <u>aboard</u>."

____ N. Put the groceries in a paper <u>bag</u>.

____ O. <u>Rhubarb</u> pie is delicious.

____ P. He was in the hospital after riding the mechanical <u>bull</u>.

1. a cut at the ball

2. where the teams at bat in baseball stay

3. a mistake on the part of the pitcher

4. when a ball is hit out of play

5. after a batter hits deep to an outfielder and the ball is caught

6. a player in the American League who only bats

7. after reaching first base a player advances to second with no help from the next batter

8. the cheap seats in a baseball park

9. a fast pitch that goes right past a batter and is called a strike

10. when an outfielder races to catch a ball and grabs it just before it hits the ground

11. a term describing a runner on base

12. a fight on the field

13. pitchers warm up in the _____ pen

14. the player currently at bat

15. another name for base

16. where the pitcher throws from

Answers, page 157

Speaking of Baseball

Sport: Baseball

Purpose: To expand a student's use of figurative language by introducing certain phrases from baseball that have infiltrated our everyday speech.

Materials: Pencils, paper

Discussion: Many sports, including baseball, have provided expressions that lend descriptions to everyday situations. Developing an understanding of figurative expressions will strengthen critical comprehension skills.

Directions: In the spaces provided after each sentence listed below, have the student use the words underlined to develop a sentence in the context of baseball. Then discuss the usages of the terms in both the example and the student's sentence.

1. The elderly lady was a hit in her first appearance on stage.

   _____

2. I suppose my neighbor has struck out once again trying to harvest his wheat before the rainy season._____

   _____

3. A young lady in the debate club told me I was way off base with my radical views of politics._____

   _____

4. "Don't get caught off base!" my friend warned, as I entered the garage without a weapon to check on the strange noise. _____

   _____

5. That barber is in left field when it comes to styling men's hair.

   _____

6. Tire companies make their pitches to sell more tires at certain times of the year._____

   _____

7. "Elliot's decision to stay with the sinking boat was a blooper!" declared the ship's captain._____

   _____

8. Bonnie felt like the victim of a squeeze play after talking to her mother and grandmother about joining the cheerleaders club.

_____

9. The first horse was already in the starting gate, but Pleasant Colony was still warming up. _____

_____

10. During the ceremony, the speaker tried to cover all his bases with a well-rehearsed speech on economics._____

_____

11. Thinking about the morning's activities at my new job makes me want to call the manager and tell him I am out of his league.

_____

12. The prisoner told the sheriff he was ready to play ball after the officer had locked the cell._____

_____

13. The attempt to free the horses failed once more, and the cowboys now had 2 strikes against them._____

_____

14. The fact that Ralph got so much attention for his rabbit trick was considered a grandstand play by the rest of us._____

_____

15. I'd like to take a rain check on that dinner invitation. _____

_____

16. Larry Holmes knocked out Leon Spinks right off the bat! _____

_____

17. "I'll throw you a curve this time," thought the bartender as he made the customer's next drink._____

_____

18. "That clown certainly has a lot on the ball for moving away from the falling ladder," I thought to myself._____

_____

19. If we want to attend the party next Saturday, we need some <u>teamwork</u> to get this job done first. _____

Follow-Up Activity: Have the student match the word or phrase in column 2 with the description in column 1.

___ 1. a hit

___ 2. struck out

___ 3. never gets to first base

___ 4. way off base

___ 5. caught off base

___ 6. out in left field

___ 7. make pitches

___ 8. blooper

___ 9. victim of a squeeze play

___ 10. still warming up

___ 11. cover all bases

___ 12. out of your league

___ 13. ready to play ball

___ 14. 2 strikes against them

___ 15. a grandstand play

___ 16. a rain check

___ 17. right off the bat

___ 18. thrown you a curve

___ 19. on the ball

___ 20. teamwork

A. When people of 2 differing views are pressuring you, then you are the _____.

B. When a person deals with a situation thoroughly, s/he is said to _____.

C. A successful person or event is _____.

D. People who have made serious mistakes or "missed the mark" badly are said to be _____.

E. When you are just getting started, you are _____.

F. Someone who is not very lucky has _____.

G. When you are with people more capable than you, you are _____.

H. Someone who tries to succeed with something or somebody else, but can't _____.

I. An unexpected turn of events means you probably were _____.

J. A person who makes an enthusiastic attempt to influence another's opinion or judgment _____.

K. Someone who acts zany is _____.

L. A silly or foolish mistake is a _____.

M. When something happens instantly, it is said to have occurred _____.

N. Someone who is alert is _____.

O. Someone willing to cooperate is _____.

P. When a group of people work together toward a common goal, that is _____.

Q. Someone who asks you a question that you are not prepared to answer has _____.

R. A person who does something for the sole purpose of letting others see the act is making _____.

S. Those who go into something without a good chance of success have _____.

T. When an event is cancelled, and tickets for an alternate date are issued, you receive _____.

Answers, page 157

Word Meanings in Sports

Sport: Basketball

Purpose: To develop a student's vocabulary by introducing words related to basketball but which may be used in a different context to mean something else; to improve a student's ability to write sentences using words which have more than one meaning.

Materials: Pencil, paper

Discussion: Parents and teachers can make good use of sports-related newspaper or magazine articles to help students pick out key multiple-meaning words. Understanding the meanings of words in different contexts is a vital reading skill. Many students have a tendency to apply only one meaning to various words. This inflexible approach to vocabulary limits their ability to read critically and often creates confusion and misunderstanding.

Directions: Ask the student to read the 9 sentences on the following page silently and find and underline key words related to basketball. Allow approximately 5 minutes for this activity. Before the student begins the activity, use the following examples to illustrate how certain words used in one context can be used to mean something entirely different in another.

Baseball—How long will the strike by the truck drivers go on?
    The umpire called the first pitch a strike.

Golf—I could tell he was teed off at me.
    The leader in that tournament teed off on the 18th hole with the victory already at hand.

Basketball—Pick a good partner and go out and enjoy yourself.
    The guard set a pick that allowed the forward to score easily.

Show the youngster that each underlined word takes on a different meaning in these sentences. Finally, ask the child to read the directions above and complete the activity.

1. I always work overtime at my job.
2. My brother said, "Please pass the gravy."
3. The horse became nervous in his stall.
4. We sat in the center of the room.
5. His occupation was that of a traveling salesman.
6. Please step forward when your name is called.

7. The net profits for the year totaled one million dollars.

8. Let's go back to the court and play a few more sets of tennis.

9. Will you please press these slacks?

After the student has read the sentences and underlined the words associated with basketball, have him/her use the words below in sentences related to another sporting event or game:

> Example: foul—The foul occurred at center ice—hockey.

1. overtime— _____

_____

2. pass— _____

3. stall— _____

_____

4. center— _____

_____

5. traveling— _____

_____

6. forward— _____

_____

7. net— _____

_____

8. court— _____

_____

9. press— _____

_____

Answers, page 157

Follow-Up Activity: In basketball, as well as in other sports, there are certain phrases that describe a specific part of the game. Below are 9 phrases pertaining to basketball. In the blank spaces below, have the student write his/her interpretations of the underlined phrases.

1. The coach's antics earned him a "T." _____

_____

2. Jack Hays, the team's leading scorer, definitely has the soft touch.

_____

_____

3. They have a <u>run-and-gun</u> offense. _____

_____

4. That shot hit <u>nothing</u> <u>but net</u>. _____

_____

5. Larry Bird is a <u>clutch</u> <u>player</u>. _____

_____

6. The Spurs won because they <u>dominated</u> <u>the</u> <u>boards</u>. _____

_____

7. I admire him because he is <u>an</u> <u>unselfish</u> <u>player</u>. _____

_____

8. <u>"In your face"</u> basketball is exciting to watch. _____

_____

9. Kareem's <u>sky-hook</u> is impossible to stop. _____

_____

Answers, page 157

NFL Search and Find

Sport:	Football
Purpose:	To develop a student's ability to follow directions; to recognize words; to improve his/her perception.
Materials:	Set of directions, puzzles, pencil.
Discussion:	Students can develop their powers of concentration and visual-reading strengths by locating and circling the nicknames of football teams hidden in search-and-find puzzles. A student's ability to follow directions can be enhanced by providing written directions for the student to read and follow. If the student's football knowledge is limited, the list of nicknames can be provided with the puzzle.
Directions:	Locate and circle the hidden nicknames of the 14 American Football Conference teams in this puzzle. Answers can be found horizontally, vertically, diagonally, forward, or backward. Then write the answers in the blanks provided below.

```
R  U  G  V  E  O  I  P  K  H  F  S  W  Q  C  M  I  L  O
S  C  U  I  O  P  R  Q  S  H  J  K  L  B  D  R  Y  U  Y
B  R  O  N  C  O  S  O  I  F  C  R  E  W  L  M  N  V  V
D  G  A  V  C  O  O  U  S  U  S  L  A  G  N  E  B  F  W
L  S  U  I  Y  H  J  O  P  R  S  F  E  I  H  C  D  F  J
O  P  E  B  D  D  I  B  Q  U  E  N  E  X  O  O  H  D  B
V  B  U  I  O  E  Q  H  B  M  E  L  S  K  O  L  Q  S  R
S  G  R  G  V  S  R  H  I  O  P  H  I  S  Q  T  G  R  O
F  K  P  O  M  L  H  S  P  A  T  R  I  O  T  S  C  E  W
E  V  W  V  B  T  S  T  E  E  L  E  R  S  G  H  Y  G  N
R  G  B  A  N  I  T  Y  U  I  D  B  X  V  W  D  T  R  S
G  F  N  I  H  O  L  R  S  T  E  J  S  B  T  Y  U  A  I
R  G  B  Y  U  A  F  L  G  B  N  W  T  D  G  V  C  H  S
D  Y  U  I  O  P  E  H  S  F  W  D  C  B  S  E  T  C  G
E  R  T  N  J  I  O  S  P  D  O  L  P  H  I  N  S  F  H
D  E  Y  U  I  O  P  J  D  Q  F  V  H  U  I  K  O  F  E
E  R  T  Y  U  I  N  D  Q  I  O  P  F  C  S  H  N  I  O
```

Answers, page 158

Locate and circle the hidden nicknames of the 14 National Football Conference teams in this puzzle. Answers can be found horizontally, vertically, diagonally, forward, or backward. Then write the answers in the blanks provided below.

```
A  F  W  K  L  C  V  Q  I  S  H  N  W  O  P  O  V  A  O
K  U  F  O  R  T  Y  N  I  N  E  R  S  O  I  I  H  B  Q
G  L  D  C  E  Y  U  I  B  O  A  L  P  F  K  F  S  D  W
D  I  Y  X  C  I  O  P  S  D  G  N  Y  I  F  Q  Y  I  O
D  C  A  Y  R  V  U  I  N  P  L  W  N  C  V  Y  B  H  I
D  S  T  N  I  A  S  S  O  I  E  G  V  N  Q  U  E  D  I
K  F  V  Y  T  I  X  C  C  Y  S  H  I  O  P  Q  A  F  C
V  C  F  G  N  S  V  C  L  T  Y  K  F  Q  Y  O  R  B  Z
F  O  U  A  F  B  P  O  A  K  P  A  C  K  E  R  S  M  L
R  W  F  H  Y  L  T  W  F  W  B  J  S  Y  Y  R  J  M  O
K  B  B  T  I  O  C  B  U  C  C  A  N  E  E  R  S  M  P
P  O  K  N  B  K  O  O  H  Y  I  O  I  N  T  V  C  E  U
P  Y  I  K  S  M  A  R  N  K  L  L  K  U  G  F  D  B  I
O  S  L  J  N  U  R  D  S  S  I  P  S  H  K  N  R  B  W
J  L  P  K  O  K  R  G  V  C  A  R  D  I  N  A  L  S  Q
O  L  F  W  I  B  H  U  O  F  D  E  E  N  P  W  Q  D  U
P  D  W  N  L  M  L  E  W  D  Y  I  R  O  H  G  F  R  D
```

Answers, page 158

Follow-Up Activity:

Ask the student to write in the spaces below, the cities or states where the National Football League teams are located.

AMERICAN FOOTBALL CONFERENCE

1. Patriots _____
2. Dolphins _____
3. Jets _____
4. Bills _____
5. Colts _____
6. Steelers _____
7. Oilers _____

8. Browns _____

9. Bengals _____

10. Broncos _____

11. Raiders _____

12. Seahawks _____

13. Chargers _____

14. Chiefs _____

NATIONAL FOOTBALL CONFERENCE

1. Saints _____

2. Forty Niners _____

3. Cowboys _____

4. Eagles _____

5. Redskins _____

6. Cardinals _____

7. Giants _____

8. Vikings _____

9. Packers _____

10. Lions _____

11. Bears _____

12. Buccaneers _____

13. Rams _____

14. Falcons _____

Answers, page 159

Para-graphs

Sport: Football

Purpose: To locate information on a graph; to improve a student's ability to interpret pictorial information.

Materials: Paper, pencil

Discussion: Frequently, students must read and locate information by using graphs. Parents and teachers can stimulate students' understanding and interpretation of graphically illustrated material using sports data.

Directions: Ask the student to study the following graphs and answer the following questions regarding the Cowboys' play in 1979 and 1980:

1. How many more games were won in August 1980 than in August 1979?_____ in October 1979?_____

2. What was the difference between the number of games won during January 1979 and January 1980?_____ What is the difference between September 1979 and September 1980?_____

3. In which month was there no gain nor loss?_____

4. During which months of the 1979 season were the same number of games won? (2 answers)_____ in 1980? (2 answers)_____ Were more games won in 1979 or 1980?_____

5. Which month(s) did the team win the most games in 1979?_____ in 1980?_____ In which month(s) did the team win the least games in 1979?_____ in 1980?_____

Answers, page 159

1979 DALLAS COWBOYS

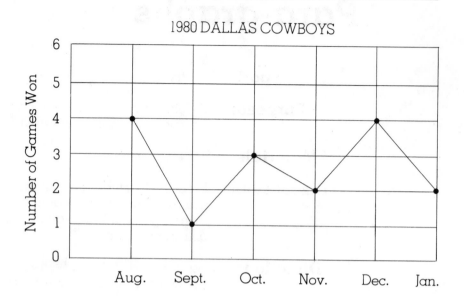

1980 DALLAS COWBOYS

Ask the student to study the following 2 bar graphs and answer the accompanying questions.

Follow-Up Activity:

1. How many more passes did Drew Pearson catch in 1980 than in 1979?_____
   Which receiver caught exactly 30 passes in 1979?_____;
   20 passes in 1979?_____

2. What is the difference between the number of passes caught by Jay Saldi and by Butch Johnson in 1979?_____

3. What is the total number of passes caught by the 5 receivers in both 1979 and 1980?_____

4. What is the total number of passes caught by Robert Newhouse and Tony Dorsett in 1979?_____ in 1980?_____

5. Which receivers caught the fewest passes in both seasons?_____ the most in both seasons?_____

6. From the graph, was 1979 a better year for receivers or worse year for them than 1980?_____
   Why?_____

7. Which receiver showed the greatest improvement in 1980?_____ the least?_____

Answers, page 159

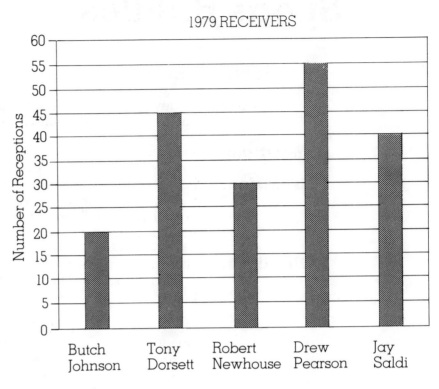

1979 RECEIVERS

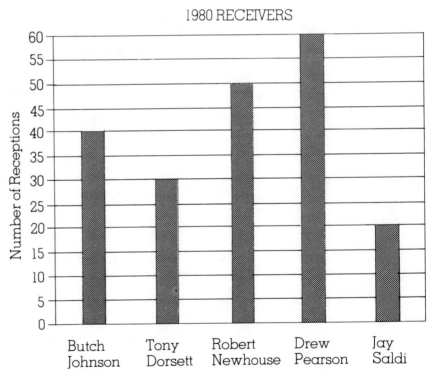

1980 RECEIVERS

Sports Riddles

Sport: Football

Purpose: To develop a student's reading and writing vocabulary and critical thinking skills through the use of various football riddles.

Materials: Pencil

Discussion: Parents and teachers can introduce riddles whose solutions represent names of football teams to encourage a student to do critical thinking. The ability to think critically is essential to becoming a good reader or writer.

Directions: Have the student write the name of the NFL team that solves the riddles that follow. The teams that serve as answers are listed below:

Buccaneers	Packers	Seahawks
Rams	Chargers	49'ers
Oilers	Steelers	Broncos
Giants	Eagles	Redskins
		Saints

1. This professional football team from southern California is electrifying because everything it has is bought on credit or _____
   _____

2. This professional football team from Colorado does not horse around! _____
   _____

3. This professional football team from Texas is just like "black gold."
   _____

4. This pro football team from Florida is worth its weight in corn, one buck an ear. _____
   _____

5. This pro football team from Washington, DC always appears to be sunburned. _____
   _____

6. This pro team from Pennsylvania soars high over America.
   _____

7. This pro team from California is often rambunctuous. _____

8. The fans of this professional team in Louisiana are guilty of hagiolatry. _____

9. This pro football team from Pennsylvania will purloin your attention. _____

10. This pro football team from Wisconsin is said to pack it away at the training table. _____

11. This pro football team in New York is a gargantuan competitor. _____

12. This California pro football team takes its name from the wild search for a bonanza in the 19th-century United States. _____

13. This pro football team in Seattle takes it name from an ocean-going bird. _____

Answers, page 159

Follow-Up Activity: Discuss each riddle and its answer. Using the following professional football teams named, ask the student to make up riddles.

1. New York Jets
2. Los Angeles Raiders
3. Dallas Cowboys
4. Miami Dolphins
5. St. Louis Cardinals
6. Minnesota Vikings
7. Detroit Lions
8. Cincinnati Bengals
9. Cleveland Browns

What's the Meaning of All This

Sport: Football

Purpose: To develop a student's comprehension of unfamiliar vocabulary through the use of context clues.

Materials: Pencil, paper, sports-related story

Discussion: Articles that appear in the sports section of the newspaper frequently contain words and expressions that are unfamiliar to many students. Students should learn that there are certain aids to getting the meaning of words without going to the dictionary or asking another person for the definitions. One way of establishing the meaning of unknown words is to make use of context clues. Context clues are words or phrases in a sentence that help the student understand the meaning of an unfamiliar word or expression. Sometimes context clues may appear in a sentence that comes before or after the one that contains the unfamiliar term(s).

Directions: Ask the student to read the following sports story, paying particular attention to the underlined words. Allow 5-10 minutes for the student to read the story silently. Then, discuss the various contextual clues used by the author to define unfamiliar words. Use the following example to introduce context clues to the student:

> The Bears' split end, Bob Taylor, a receiver coming off the line of scrimmage, made a phenomenal grab at the 30-yard line. This unbelievable catch allowed Taylor's team to finish the season with a clean slate.

Discuss the meaning of "split end" in terms of the context clue in the first sentence (a receiver coming off the line of scrimmage) which defines it. Do the same for "phenomenal," showing the youngster how the word "unbelievable" in the next sentence provides a key for understanding this term. Tell the student that context clues such as these help give a clearer idea of what the terms "split end" and "phenomenal" mean. Have the student reread the sports article for the purpose of finding context clues for the underlined words. Then, have the student complete the exercises on the following pages.

SOUTH EDGES NORTH, 20-17

   The South All-Stars clipped the North All-Stars Saturday night in a game that was not determined until the final play.
   Jack Fisher, the South's kick-return specialist, took the opening kickoff at the 15, evaded 2 tacklers by side-stepping them at the 25, and raced the remaining 75 yards to paydirt for the South's first touchdown.

However, the North was not to be outdone. Clyde Moss took the following kickoff and sprinted down the right sideline for the North's first score. This return was a <u>duplicate</u> of the earlier return by the South, because it was an exact copy in terms of yards covered.

The score stood at 7–7 until Mike Lee of the North scored on a one-yard dive to make the score 13–7. James Smith's conversion attempt was <u>true</u> as the ball split the uprights to give the North a 14–7 advantage.

The South All-Stars covered 80 yards in 15 plays late in the second quarter. Jeff Phipps' 4-yard run and Anderson's second successful conversion were the result of this long drive. As the first half ended, both teams entered their dressing rooms in a <u>deadlock</u>. The score was tied, 14–14.

Neither team scored in the third quarter. There were numerous <u>miscues</u>. The third quarter was plagued by penalties, costly fumbles, and interceptions.

The first 3 plays of the fourth quarter proved costly for the South team. On the <u>initial</u> series of downs of the final period, the South lost yardage on first and second down. Then, on third down quarterback Ron Lynn was intercepted by North linebacker Grant Jones on the South 35-yard line.

On 3 <u>successive</u> tries, the North squad gained only 2 yards on first down, 1 yard on second down, and 2 yards on third down. Faced with the decision to go for the first down or kick a field goal, North coach Bill Lowe chose the <u>latter</u>. Smith's 29-yard field goal gave the North a 17–14 edge.

However, the South proved that they could rise again. With 9 seconds left in the game, the South had 36 yards to go for the game winner. The <u>finale</u> was spectacular as end Tom Green caught the touchdown pass on the last play of the game. The South won the game 20–17.

Have the student define below the underlined terms in his/her own words. Then have him/her write the words, phrases, or sentences that appear in the story and serve as contextual aids in establishing the meaning of each term.

1. evaded

   context clues: _____

   _____

2. paydirt

   context clues: _____

   _____

3. duplicate

   context clues: _____

   _____

4. true

context clues: _____

_____

5. deadlock

context clues: _____

_____

6. miscues

context clues: _____

_____

7. initial

context clues: _____

_____

8. successive

context clues: _____

_____

9. latter

context clues: _____

_____

10. finale

context clues: _____

_____

Answers, page 159

Follow-Up Activity:

In column 1 are 10 names that have been made up but give a hint to a certain player's position in football. In column 2 are the actual football positions. Match the letters in column 2 to the fictitious names in column 1.

____	A.	Frank Hike	1.	linebacker
____	B.	Tom Receiver	2.	fullback
____	C.	Ican Bootit	3.	quarterback
____	D.	Ron Withaball	4.	guard
____	E.	Will Stopyou	5.	end
____	F.	Harvey Playmaker	6.	safety
____	G.	Rich Sentry	7.	place kicker
____	H.	Joe T. Itup	8.	punter
____	I.	I.C. Thepass	9.	center
____	J.	Ryan Runback	10.	kick-return specialist

Answers, page 160

Swing into Paragraphs

Sport: Golf

Purpose: To develop a student's understanding and use of the elements of paragraph writing.

Materials: Paper, pencil, paragraph about golf

Discussion: Being able to construct a good paragraph is a prerequisite to writing an essay. While paragraphs represent the separate "building blocks" of a longer section of material, they also encompass the basic elements of a well-written essay in compact form. These features are the introduction of the main idea (topic sentence), logical organization of ideas, transition words to tie ideas together, and a conclusion which summarizes or restates the main idea. This activity leads the student to discover these elements and then use them in writing an original paragraph. It should be noted that this activity does not teach a student everything s/he needs to know about paragraph writing; rather, it introduces him/her to a basic form which will aid in further development of general writing skills.

Directions: Give a copy of the following paragraph to the student and have him/her point out the following:

1. Topic sentence—a statement that expresses the main idea.
2. Logical organization of ideas—a generally accepted or appropriate order that indicates when, where, how, or why events happen. (Example: The door opened. The man walked in. Everyone stood up. They all applauded.)
3. Transition words— words that help sentences flow together smoothly.
4. Conclusion—ends the paragraph by summing up or restating the main idea.

If the student has trouble locating these elements within the paragraph, give him/her the following directions. These will help develop his/her understanding:

A. Underline the first sentence and read it to yourself. Notice that it indicates what the whole paragraph is about. It is called the topic sentence and its purpose is to introduce the reader to the main idea of this paragraph.

B. Notice that there is a logical order for the appearance of each step in the following paragraph. These are presented consecutively from the first to the last.

C. Now circle the words first of all, then, now, and finally. (Allow the student ample time to do this.) These are called transition words, and they help the paragraph move smoothly from one idea to the next.

D.   Next, have the student underline the last sentence and compare it to the first sentence. Ask the student to explain any differences and/or similarities.

E.   Finally, review the paragraph elements and ask the student to explain what the topic sentence, transition words, and conclusion are. Ask him/her to discuss the logical organization of the paragraph's ideas.

THE GOLF SWING

Making a good golf shot requires following some fundamental steps. First of all, you must have an overlapping, comfortable grip on the club. Then, start your backswing by bringing your club straight back from the ball. Be sure to have your knees flexed, your eye on the ball, and try not to dip your shoulder. Now, hit the ball by bringing the club back through the same arc while shifting your weight from right to left (if you're right-handed). Finally, continue the swing after the club hits the ball until your hands are back above your left shoulder. It is important to follow these basic rules if you want to develop a good golf swing.

Follow-Up Activity: The student can learn to write a good paragraph by following the steps from the preceding activity. To help him/her accomplish this, use the following directions as a guide:

1.   The first step in writing a good paragraph requires you to select a topic. Choose something you can do well from the world of sports and pretend you are going to describe for someone else exactly how to do it (examples: how to shoot a basketball, how to catch a football, or how to throw a punch).

2.   Make a list of each step involved in completing the action. You may write these as they occur to you.

3.   Now look your list over and arrange the steps in a logical sequence such as first to last or most important to least important.

4.   Next, compose a topic sentence for your paragraph. Remember that the topic sentence lets the reader know exactly what s/he will be reading about. Refer back to the topic sentence in "The Golf Swing" if necessary.

5.   You are ready to write your first draft, but be sure to:

a. Start with a topic sentence.

b. Discuss the steps for doing whatever you have chosen to describe in a logical order.

c. Use transition words like "first," "next," "then," " after," "that," etc. to make your ideas flow smoothly. Try to avoid using terms repetitively.

d. Make the last sentence of your paragraph a conclusion that restates the topic sentence using different words.

6. Now read over the first draft of your paragraph and be sure it makes sense, follows the correct form, and contains correct punctuation, spelling, and grammar. At this point, the parent and teacher may wish to aid the student in proofreading his/her work.

7. Rewrite your paragraph making all the necessary changes and give it a title!

8. When the student has finished writing the final draft of his/her paragraph, ask him/her to point out the topic sentence, logical organization of ideas, transition words, and conclusion. This will reinforce these ideas.

Name That Horse

Sport: Horse Racing

Purpose: To show students ways to use context in order to classify information, thus improving comprehension skills.

Materials: Newspaper clippings that report horse races (one is included for this activity), pen, paper divided into 3 columns

Discussion: Understanding what is read often depends on a student's ability to use context clues—the parts of a sentence immediately next to or surrounding a specified word that determines its meaning. News reports of horse races provide an excellent opportunity for students to develop an ability to classify or group items or ideas into categories. The ability to form generalizations and make discriminations when reading adds greatly to a student's comprehension.

Directions: Give students the following sentence to read: "Velasquez's first ride aboard Pleasant Colony came in the Kentucky Derby, when he defeated a fast-closing Woodchopper by three-quarters of a length in the 21-horse field." From this sample sentence, ask the student to identify the name of the jockey, the name of the horse, and the name of the race. Discuss the context clues provided in this sentence and the information gained from the clues. For example:

1. This is Velasquez's <u>first ride</u>; therefore, he is the jockey.
2. He is <u>aboard</u> Pleasant Colony; therefore, Pleasant Colony is a horse.
3. The ride <u>came in the</u> Kentucky Derby; therefore, Kentucky Derby is the name of the race.
4. Pleasant Colony <u>defeated</u> Woodchopper who was <u>fast-closing</u>; therefore, Woodchopper is a horse.

Provide the student with a news report of a horse race. You may use the following report as an example. Also, provide the student with a sheet of paper with 3 columns labelled horses, jockeys/trainers, and horse races. Have the student read the article, then list the names that appear in the article in the appropriate column. A student may list a name more than one time if it appears in the article more than once. Discuss the answers when the exercise is completed.

Johnny Campo . . . predicted triple crown before Derby.

Belmont field could hinder Colony's bid

By Ed Schuyler Jr.
Associated Press

NEW YORK—Pleasant Colony will try to become thoroughbred racing's 12th Triple Crown champion next Saturday and to succeed, it looks as if he might have to beat more rivals than any of the others who accomplished the feat.

The colt, whose trainer, John Campo, predicted he would win the Triple Crown even before the Kentucky Derby, could have at least 11 rivals in the 11/2-mile Belmont Stakes at Belmont Park.

Citation and Seattle Slew each beat seven other 3-year-olds in the Belmont; War Admiral and Assault each beat six; Omaha, Secretariat and Affirmed defeated four apiece; Gallant Fox and Whirlaway beat three each, and Sir Barton and Count Fleet each beat two.

In fact, the biggest field in 112 Belmonts has been in 14 in 1875 when Calvin beat Derby winner Aristides. Three Belmonts each have had 13

starters—1877 when Cloverbrook won; 1954 when High Gun won, and 1971 when Pass Catcher won as Canonero II failed to win the Triple Crown.

The last two Belmonts were won by colts who had not been nominated and had to be made supplemental entries—Coastal who upset Spectacular Bid in 1979 and Temperence Hill, who beat the filly Genuine Risk last year.

At least one Belmont probable, Paristo, the Illinois Derby winner who finished third in the Preakness as a supplemental entry, would have to be supplemented. Another could be Television Studio, the Derby fifth-place finisher, who was scheduled to run Saturday in the $100,000-added Sheridan at Arlington Park. It costs $20,000 to supplement— $5,000 to nominate and $15,000 to start.

Three colts who chased Pleasant Colony home in the 11/4-mile Kentucky Derby and the 1 3/16th-mile Preakness are expected to try him again in the Belmont. They are Bold Ego, 10th in the Derby and second in the Preakness; Woodchopper, the Derby runner-up who was 11th in the Preakness and Partez,

third in the Derby and fifth in the Preakness.

Other veterans of Triple Crown competition who are Belmont probables include Tap Shoes, who was 14th in the Derby and the winner of the 11/8-mile Peter Pan May 24 at Belmont, and Highland Blade, Escambia Bay and Bare Knuckles, who ran 6-7-8, respectively, in the Preakness.

Two other Belmont prospects are Summing, who won the Pennsylvania Derby at Keystone May 25 and paid $72.50, and Shahnameh, who finished eighth in the Blue Grass Stakes.

Should Pleasant Colony, owned by Thomas Mellon Evans and ridden by Jorge Velasquez, lose in the Belmont, he would become the 10th to miss the Triple Crown after having won the Kentucky Derby and Preakness.

The nine who failed were Pensive, 1944; Tim Tam, 1958; Carry Back, 1961; Northern Dancer, 1964; Kauai King, 1966; Forward Pass, 1968; Majestic Prince, 1969; Canonero II and Spectacular Bid.

Horses	Jockeys/Trainers	Horse Races

Follow-Up Activity:

To reinforce a student's classification skills, use the following activity. In this make-believe horse race, each student becomes a jockey. Each jockey chooses a name for the horse s/he rides. The horse whose jockey correctly completes the following activity in the shortest time wins the race.

Howard Cosell is a roving sportscaster who goes from one sports event to another to report special events to sports fans. Read the following comments made by Mr. Cosell and determine what sport he was reporting at the time. Write the name of the sport in the blank provided after each quotation.

"We have just finished seeing Palmer shoot an eagle on the thirty-sixth hole. His caddie is now leaving the green."

_____

"He scored the extra point by making a superb drop kick. The score is now 7-0. The defensive unit is rushing onto the field."

_____

"The mounts used in this event are quite valuable. The challenge is to ride a mount equipped only with a leather surcingle, or rigging, around its middle. He's done it! The 10-second buzzer has just sounded!"

_____

"This bout will determine the featherweight championship. That was a very effective duck to avoid the opponent's right hook intended for the jaw."

_____

"It appears we have a shutout game, and the players in the dugout are obviously jubilant."

_____

"Standing 7' 2", he is one of the greatest offensive players in the history of the game. Jackson is a real pro with this faking technique. And here he comes with a pivot! He's made a good shot for a score!"

_____

"Here at the start of the final round of the Davis Cup competition, we have just witnessed the most inundating display of overhand smashes of this century."

_____

"The defensive players are seeking to break up the invasion of their territory. The goalkeeper is executing his privileges inside the penalty area to stop the ball from scoring."

"The rusher came from the outside, but there was splendid pass protection. The quarterback managed to get the pass off in the direction of a receiver."

"This dribbling offensive player has managed to drive his guard back near the goal. Now, he leaps and sinks a one-hander over the guard's head."

"That 17-year-old phenomenon shot 4 consecutive rounds of 67, 71, 72, and 71 that totaled 8 strokes under par for the course. What a tournament!"

Answers, page 160

Straight from the Horse's Mouth

Sport: Horse Racing

Purpose: To develop comprehension by introducing colorful or figurative expressions; to point out the author's use of context clues to define these terms; to improve creative writing ability by using figurative expressions.

Materials: Pencils, paper, sports-related newspaper article

Discussion: Frequently, an author will use figurative or colorful language to enhance the meaning of his/her story. When a reader is puzzled by unfamiliar language, s/he may be able to determine an author's meaning by investigating the words that surround figurative expression to comprehend their context. The following exercise will give the opportunity to find colorful and figurative language and then determine its meaning in context.

Directions: Ask the student to survey the headline and the newspaper article that follow and circle or underline colorful and descriptive phrases that may be unfamiliar. Five to 7 minutes should be sufficient for this preview. If assistance is needed in identifying the colorful expressions, help the student to locate and underline the special terminology. Then discuss the author's use of figurative expressions in place of less imaginative ones to help the student see how these add more interest to the writer's story. After the discussion, ask the student to read the article silently and complete the exercises on the following pages. Below is a list of some figurative expressions used in the article:

1. fast gun
2. fought off a wilting attack
3. pulled out a head victory
4. Triple Crown journey
5. victory slice
6. she came flying
7. The pilot is
8. the top money line
9. centered their mutuel attentions
10. mustered a brisk charge
11. carried odds of better than 9–1
12. from the rail slot
13. broke a bit sluggishly
14. bore in a bit
15. a 15–1 longshot

16. appeared to be in the bag
17. shifted into high gear
18. pieced together a tremendous charge
19. appeared ready to nail
20. she ran out of ground

★★★★★★★★★★★★★★★★★★★★★★★★★★★★★★★★★★★★★★★
RACING
★★★★★★★★★★★★★★★★★★★★★★★★★★★★★★★★★★★★★★★
Ruidoso Downs

Easily Smashed in Narrow Kansas Derby Win

Ruidoso Downs, N.M.—Easily Smashed fought off a wilting attack from Runnin Barre and pulled out a head victory in the 7th running of the Kansas Derby at Ruidoso Downs.

The Kansas Derby, the first stop on the Triple Crown journey for three-year-olds, offered a gross purse of $224,740. The victory slice amounted to $76,909. The amount distributed in the finale alone was $187,657 (plus a $5,000 breeder's award).

Easily Smashed, who performed in the 400-yard Derby as a 2-1 favorite, is owned by the partnership of Carl Childs, William Leach and Sue May of Ft. Stockton, TX. Leach also trains the colt. The pilot is Jackie Martin.

The winning time of 20.09 seconds (a seasonal record) was a considerable improvement over Easy Joni Jet's top-qualifying time of 20.34. The qualifying trials, however, were run under extremely windy conditions. The conditions for the May 24 Derby finale were perfect. It was a clear, sunny afternoon, with only a slight, occasional breeze.

Although Easily Smashed qualified 10th best, Ruidoso patrons figured he was still the one to beat, and made him the choice in the finale. His big selling point was a two-length win in the trials, plus the top money line of close to $160,000.

Fans who centered their mutuel attentions on Easily Smashed in the Kansas Derby collected $6, $3.69 and $3. The son of Easy Jet out of Smash It

came out of the Derby with a perfect '81 record of three-for-three. Last year, he compiled outstanding marks of 9-2-0 from 13 outings.

Runnin Barre, ridden by Steve Treasure for Robert and Juanita Ballenger of Paoli, OK., banked $35,158 for his runner-up effort. The tote returns were $3.80 and $3.40. Easy Joni Jet owned by Louie Allen of Allen, TX., mustered a brisk charge in the final stages but had to settle for third, a neck behind Runnin Barre. The show price was $4. Easy Joni Jet carried odds of better than 9-1. The third-place paycheck amounted to $18,018.

Easily Smashed got off to a strong get-away from the rail slot and quickly assumed command. Mighty Pass Em, Easy Joni Jet and Moon Chicks quickly got into some tight quarters from the Nos. 1, 3, and 4 posts. Runnin Barre broke a bit sluggishly and bore in a bit.

Easily Smashed was clearly in charge when he was about 100 yards away from the gate, although some arguments were delivered by Native Tea, a 15-1 longshot. Just when things appeared to be in the bag for Easily Smashed, Runnin Barre shifted into high gear on the far outside. She pieced together a tremendous charge and appeared ready to nail Easily Smashed when she ran out of ground.

For Easily Smashed, the win was his first major victory since his conquest of the $250,388 Sun Country Futurity at Sunland Park in the spring of 1980.

Here's how the also-rans checked in for the Kansas Derby: 4th-Ooh Lala Lala, earning $9,448; 5th-Native Tea, $8,569; 6th-Moses Lad, $8,350; 7th-Mighty Pass Em, $8,130; 8th-El Rey Burner, $7,910; 9th-Pajaro Chick, $7,960; and 10th-Moon Chicks, $7,471.

Moon Chicks lost a stirrup during the race.

Jockey Martin sized up the victory in this way: "Easily Smashed is just a super horse. He was ahead about a length 1,000 yards away from the gate. Then we came over the hump leading onto the main track, and he kind of stumbled. I picked him up and he started running real hard. They were coming pretty hard at us in the last 100 yards.

Martin had his choice of four horses to ride in the Derby finale, and opted for Easily Smashed—despite the colt's bottom qualifying time. "Easily Smashed was good to me last year with more than $150,000 in winnings and I thought he'd run a strong race in the Derby," he explained. "In the trials, he ran against a head wind, so his time didn't bother me."

Martin's three other qualifiers were Runnin Barre, Moses Lad and Ooh Lala Lala.

Steve Treasurer, the fast gun who was imported to handle Runnin Barre, observed: "She broke in a little and I took hold. Then she came flying. I'm sure she lost a little ground at the start."

Have the student write a brief interpretation of the expressions below.

1. fast gun _____

2. fought off a wilting attack _____

3. pulled out a head victory _____

4. Triple Crown journey _____

5. victory slice _____

6. broke a bit sluggishly _____

7. appeared ready to nail _____

8. the top money line _____

9. centered their mutuel attentions _____

10. mustered a brisk charge _____

11. she ran out of ground _____

12. shifted into high gear _____

Answers, page 160

Follow-Up Activity: Using the following "kernel" phrases, ask the student to write colorful expressions and descriptors that help expand or refine each phrase into a clear, complete statement as in the following example:

> picked him up—Suddenly realizing the magnitude of the situation, I picked him up and started pounding leather.

1. a 15–1 longshot _____

2. from the rail position _____

3. the jockey is _____

4. picked up the pace _____

5. suddenly closed in _____

6. ran against a head wind _____

7. the betting favorite of the day _____

8. got off to a strong start _____

Time Signals

Sport: Horse Racing

Purpose: To develop a student's comprehension by introducing time-related signal words that sequence the order of events in an article on horse racing.

Materials: Paper, pencils, newspaper or magazine article related to horse racing

Discussion: Time-related signal words are important because they indicate the order in which various events occur in an article or story. Parents and teachers can make good use of sports-related newspaper and magazine articles to introduce these terms to the student. Knowing the function these words serve in written material aids students' ability to recall events according to their appearance in the article or story and from relationships among the ideas, events, and subjects.

Directions: Below are some time-signal words that are used in the sports article that follows. Review these terms, then read the headline and article for the purpose of circling or underlining the various signal words and terms. Allow approximately 7–10 minutes for the student to complete this exercise. Afterwards, discuss a few of the words or terms with the student and point out that time-related signal words are indispensable for learning the sequence of events and establishing relationships in the content of various written material. Finally, ask the student to complete the exercises on the following pages.

1. 14th time
2. starts
3. after running
4. that afternoon
5. always
6. before the race
7. has often
8. past 6
9. At the December 23 race
10. then
11. began picking
12. too early
13. finishing second
14. first for
15. sixth place
16. finisher
17. starting spot
18. next year's

Answers, page 161

Have the student copy all of the sentences from the article which contain time-related signal words. The results should be a paraphrase of the article as well as the sequence of events presented in the material. Use the blank space below to complete this activity.

Starting with: Winning for the 14th time out of her 20 career starts . . .

Ending with: The win entitles Miss Thermolark to a starting spot in next year's. . . .

Answers, page 162

Miss Thermolark Wins Champion of Champions

By Cathy Dixon

Winning for the 14th time out of her 20 career starts, Miss Thermolark took home the Champion of Champion's trophy after running the 440 yards in a brisk :21.65. The 1975 bay mare's speed has been surpassed in the Champion of Champions only by Dash For Cash who set the record with speeds of :21.17 and :21.62 the past two years.

Owned by Ronny Schliep of Sallisaw, Oklahoma, the new champion was under the training of highly respected Blane Schvaneveldt. Schvaneveldt, who had won three other races that afternoon said, ``We really haven't done anything differently; it's just that this horse has always been so easy to train. We thought we had a real good shot before the race and we think she should

have an excellent shot at championship honors.''

The Champion of Champions has often been a stepping-stone to the World Champion Quarter Running Horse title honor with four of the past six winners having become the world champion. If Miss Thermolark becomes the 1978 champion, she will be joining the ranks of such greats as Easy Date, Mr. Jet Moore and Dash For Cash.

At the December 23 race, Miss Thermolark broke on top and appeared to have the race won, then 27-1 longshot Native Creek showed how he earned his invitation to the prestigious race and began picking up ground. Native Creek's jockey, Richard Bickel, moved the stallion to the outside of Miss Thermolark but ran out of ground too early, finishing second by only a head.

Miss Thermolark was ridden by jockey Kenny Hart, who is second this year in number of wins, and first for the second straight year in money won. Hart said, ``She really broke well, and it enabled us to get a very easy lead. I was pretty sure we had the race won. When Native Creek came up on the outside, I just waved the whip at Miss Thermolark and she held him off,'' Hart said.

Miss Thermolark was second in the wagering to sixth place finisher Medley Glass. Miss Thermolark returned $7.40, $4.20 and $3.80, and combined with Native Creek on a $5 exacta for $393.50. The win entitles Miss Thermolark to a starting spot in next year's Champion of Champions and the $63,750 winner's purse boosted her lifetime earnings to $441,828.

The Quarter Horse Journal, January 1979, page 186

Follow-Up Activity: The following list of time-related words is taken from the article and expanded to include all the numbers between one and 10. Reading from left to right, circle the word that does not have anything to do with the first word in the row and find the saying from the track announcer. See the following example.

| eleventh | eleven | 11th | 10+1 | (not) |

1.	first	one	cent	1st	all
2.	second	2nd	pair	is	two
3.	third	triple	lost	three	3rd
4.	fourth	that	four	4th	square
5.	fifth	5th	nickel	is	five
6.	sixth	poured	hexagon	6th	6th
7.	seventh	seven	lucky 7	7th	into
8.	eighth	octagon	a	eight	8th
9.	ninth	last inning	9th	leaky	nine
10.	tenth	bucket	dime	ten	10th

Put the words which are circled on these lines to find out what the track announcer has to say.

___1___	___2___	___3___
___4___	___5___	___6___
___7___	___8___	___9___
___10___		

Answers, page 162

The Hand is Quicker than the Eye or Club

Sport: Karate

Purpose: To develop a student's understanding of the sport of karate and increase his/her vocabulary; to encourage the student to write using karate as a theme.

Materials: Introduction to karate, crossword puzzle, pen, additional reading material on the sport.

Discussion: Understanding and using a wide range of terms and expressions is important for effective communication. The world of sports offers opportunities for the students to develop broad language skills. Each sport has a vocabulary that is truly unique. Karate can serve as a source to expand a student's vocabulary by introducing him/her to words with multiple meanings. Students are eager to learn these words because karate is exciting for the student who has a wealth of vicarious experience viewing motion pictures and television programs where karate is employed.

Parents or teachers are encouraged to find books, booklets, or articles pertaining to the sport of karate. These can be used to create an interest for further reading.

Directions: Ask the student to read the following article about the sport of karate. Prior to reading the article, ask the student to preview the material by scanning the article and underlining terms that s/he may not understand. Discuss these words with the student before allowing him/her to read independently. Have the student complete the following crossword puzzle:

ACROSS

1,2. Karate routine in which participants cannot touch each other (2 words)

5. The color of the belt which indicates a person has achieved the highest honor in the sport of karate

8. Every lesson in karate begins with a _____

10. The color of a beginner's belt

11. A judge of fairness in sports

14. The meeting place for lessons in karate

18. The sport of karate teaches defense against _____

19. The Orient has given the world _____

DOWN

3. Speed is _____ in the sport of karate

4. A color that indicates an intermediate-level student of karate

5. A word that means sudden, quick attack

7. The name for a person who knows how to perform the exercises of karate

9,14. Karate may be used for a person (2 words) _____ _____

10. In karate, one must defend himself without a _____

12. Part of the body used in many karate moves

13. Another name for a challenger

15. Name for all the exercises or routines in the sport of karate

16. The skill level of a karateist may be told by his/her _____

17. Ashikubi is the name of a special _____

C
K A R A T E
R   F
O   P U Z Z L E
S   N
S
W
O
R
D

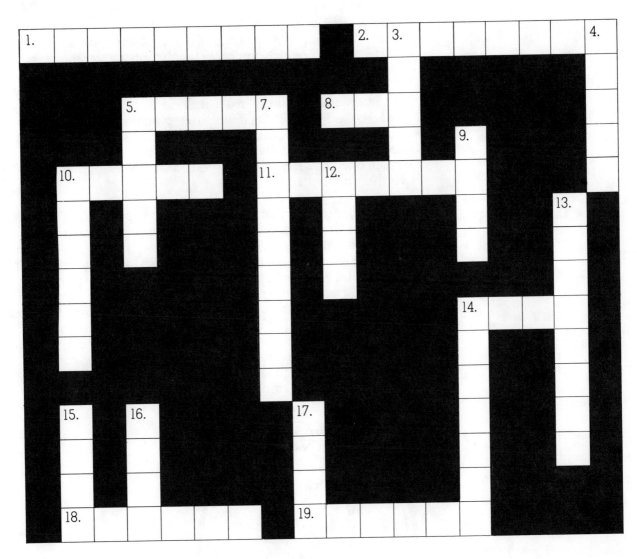

Answers, page 162

Follow-Up Activity: Ask the student to write his/her own karate story using as many of the karate terms presented in the previous activity as possible. Have the student underline these words in his/her story and discuss them.

INTRODUCTION TO KARATE

Karate is a sport which first began in the Orient. We think of the Orient as the part of the world where the countries of Japan, China, and Korea are located. Can you find any of these on a world map?

If you are a karate expert, you know how to move continuously and attack another person without using a weapon. As a matter of fact, the word *karate* means "empty hand." In karate, your feet and your fists are used for self-defense against an attacker. To be good at this sport, speed is one of the most important things. A very fast punch or kick can have much more power than a heavy weapon moving slowly.

The techniques of karate are usually learned in a special kind of school called a *dojo*. One important tradition in learning karate is to begin each lesson with the bow. This shows respect for learning the sport. Beginners wear white belts. You must earn yellow, green, and brown belts before you can attain the highest honor of wearing a black belt.

A student must learn many different ways of defense. Each exercise that a karate student learns for self-defense against an attack is called a *kata*. After a student has learned these varied ways of handling an opponent's weapons and assaults, s/he may spar with his/her teacher and other students. When combatants do freestyle sparring, they go through the motions but cannot touch each other. If they do, they lose. A referee watches the sparring and decides if the rules are followed. Two moves a karate student might learn are the *agetsuki* and the *ashikubi*. The agetsuki is an upper-cut blow delivered in an upward manner. The ashikubi is a kick delivered with the front of the ankle. Above all, remember blitzing speed is power in the sport of karate.

Answers to Middle School Section

Believe It or Not

1. lawn tennis
2. rugby
3. korfball
4. lacrosse
5. polo
6. cricket
7. rugby
8. lawn tennis
9. korfball
10. lacrosse

Information

Sports Detective WORDS WITH MULTIPLE MEANINGS

1. spare
2. stealing
3. serve
4. bullpen
5. hat trick
6. clubs
7. strike
8. single, double, triple
9. shot
10. pinch
11. love
12. short stop or shortstop
13. plate
14. chip
15. receiver
16. iron

Follow-Up Activity

	CLUE WORDS	NAME OF SPORT
1.	knocking over, 10-pins, rolls	bowling
2.	base, baseman's	baseball
3.	slice, court	tennis
4.	pitcher, warming up	baseball
5.	puck, goal	ice hockey
6.	woods, irons	golf
7.	batter, out	baseball
8.	hit, batter, first base, second base, third base	baseball
9.	one-handed jump, free throw	basketball
10.	hitter	baseball
11.	backhand stroke, thirty, match	tennis
12.	second and third base	baseball
13.	catcher, dusted-off, home	baseball
14.	shot, green	golf
15.	wide, caught, pass	football
16.	clubs	golf

Wide World of Cause and Effect A. 4, B. 7, C. 8, D. 3, E. 9, F. 1, G. 10, H. 6, I. 2, J. 5

The Hard Charger and the Bridesmaid

Cagey Yarborough wins Firecracker

By Gary Long
Knight-Ridder Wire

DAYTONA BEACH, Fla.—Cale Yarborough, hardest of the hard chargers, found himself a "gentleman race driver" Saturday and took advantage of him.

Yarborough rode the back bumper of Harry Gant's Buick most of the last 50 miles and then whipped past on the inside just one mile from the finish to win Daytona's Firecracker 400 for the fourth time.

Never a winner on the NASCAR Grand National circuit, Gant became a bridesmaid for the eighth time in the last year and a half. Nice guys finish second; but they finish.

Yarborough fully expected Gant to leave him racing room when he made his inside move at the end of the back straightway on this 2¼-mile trioval. "I know Harry Gant was the type man I didn't have to worry about," he said, meaning it as a compliment.

And what if Gant had eased down a couple grooves to try to pinch him against the infield grass? "Were you here in '79?" Yarborough responded.

The reference was to the 1979 Daytona 500. Yarborough tried the same slingshot move on Donnie Allison, again entering the third turn, again on the last lap, and Allison refused to yield.

They proceeded to bang together three times before crashing into the wall, and they ended up fighting in the third-turn infield grass while Richard Petty celebrated a gift victory.

Oddly, Petty's Buick was nipping at the heels of the frontrunners, with Buddy Baker just a few car-lengths further back, but they settled for third and fourth as Yarborough beat Gant to the line by a car-length.

"I knew if I could get into the third turn going flat-out and keep my momentum that there was no way he (Gant) could beat me back to the line," Yarborough said.

Gant, at 41 the same age as Yarborough but a relative latecomer to Grand National racing, took defeat philosophically. "There was nothing I could do to hold him off," he said. "I had tried to zig-zag across the race track to keep him from getting around me, but obviously it didn't work."

A crowd estimated at 65,000 on another of those hazy, crazy Daytona days of summer still experienced plenty of thrills without a last-lap crash for a capper.

The yellow flag flew on six occasions, slowing the field for 37 of the 160 laps, for blown engines, three single car mishaps and a wild and terrifying six-car tangle.

Yarborough, who banked $24,675 to Gant's $15,350 from a purse exceeding $260,000, appeared to have the edge in his M.C. Anderson-owned Buick. Though there were 35 official lead changes among 10 drivers, Yarborough led 78 laps.

"We've got a new set of circumstances down here," said Neil Bonnett, whose run of hard luck this season continued when the engine on his Wood Brothers Ford blew after 93 hard laps.

"The new cars (mid-sized models mandated by NASCAR this season) are really squirrelly when they're running together. If one car can break away, like Cale did, he can hold it wide open through the turns. But the guys in the pack have to back off because the cars are scooting and jumping around.

In fact, Yarborough was able to run away and leave the field in his wake twice. But after the final caution period, during which Yarborough took on four new tires, he seemed to have lost part of his advantage.

"The race track got a little greasier and my car got a little looser," he said. "I was afraid to try to break away again. You've got to use your head a little bit in this race business. It took patience, and it's hard to be patient for 30 laps. But I knew what I had to do and did it.

He and Gant swapped the lead back and forth twice. But that, Yarborough said, was just "testing" of Gant. He said, "He will win. He's got a good team."

The caution periods slowed Yarborough's average speed to 142.588 mph, a far cry from the record 173.473 winning run of Bobby Allison in the 1980 Firecracker. Allison, a four-time winner and the Grand National points leader this year, was trying to chase down Yarborough near the 275-mile mark when his engine quit.

The victory was Yarborough's 71st in an illustrious career, his second in nine 1981 events in his trimmed-back schedule.

fact-
Yarborough won the race

inference-
While it appeared Yarborough gained an early lead he lost ground in the late going.

A. Literal Comprehension
Accept any 5 of the stated facts from the article.

B. Inferential Comprehension; 1. c; 2. a; 3. b; 4. b; 5. c

Follow-Up Activity

1. false
2. true
3. true
4. false
5. false
6. true
7. false
8. true
9. true
10. false

Crossword Puzzle— American League Teams

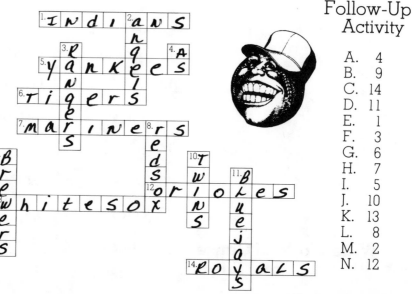

Follow-Up Activity

A. 4
B. 9
C. 14
D. 11
E. 1
F. 3
G. 6
H. 7
I. 5
J. 10
K. 13
L. 8
M. 2
N. 12

It's a Steal

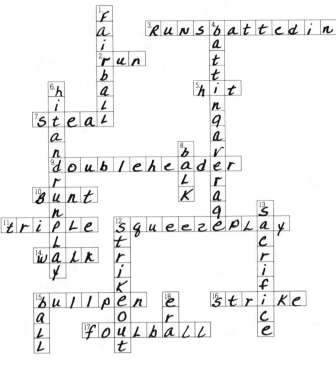

On with a Double (Meaning)

Follow-Up Activity

A.	5	E.	2	I.	8	M.	11
B.	7	F.	1	J.	9	N.	15
C.	4	G.	3	K.	14	O.	12
D.	6	H.	10	L.	16	P.	13

Speaking of Baseball Original sentences will vary.

Follow-Up Activity

A.	9	F.	2	K.	6	P.	20
B.	11	G.	12	L.	8	Q.	18
C.	1	H.	3	M.	17	R.	15
D.	4	I.	5	N.	19	S.	14
E.	10	J.	7	O.	13	T.	16

Word Meanings in Sports

1. overtime
2. pass
3. stall
4. center
5. traveling
6. forward
7. net
8. court
9. press

Follow-Up Activity

1. earned the coach a technical foul
2. a unique ability to score points or just the right "touch" when shooting baskets
3. a type of offense which is characterized by a fast-breaking style, along with shooting at will at the hoop
4. the basketball went through the net without hitting the rim or using the backboard
5. a type of player who rises to the occasion when the game is on the line or it is a key or crucial point in the game
6. had complete control of the rebounding aspect of the game

7. a player who does not try to score all of the points or one who is willing to hand out assists, pass the ball to someone who is open, or be a "team" player

8. a style of play exhibited on the playgrounds of many large cities that involves aggressive one-on-one offensive maneuverings

9. the shot used by extremely tall players whereby the arm is extended away from the body and the ball flicked toward the basket from this outstretched position

NFL Search and Find

NFC CHECKSHEET
Forty Niners
Giants
Saints
Eagles
Cardinals
Vikings
Cowboys
Bears
Lions
Rams
Falcons
Redskins
Buccaneers

AFC CHECKSHEET
Broncos
Raiders
Oilers
Bengals
Chiefs
Steelers
Patriots
Colts
Jets
Bills
Seahawks
Browns
Chargers
Dolphins

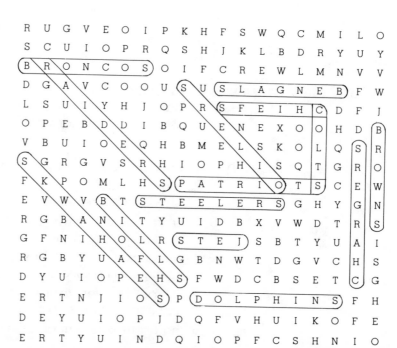

Follow-Up Activity

AMERICAN FOOTBALL CONFERENCE

1. New England; 2. Miami; 3. New York; 4. Buffalo; 5. Baltimore; 6. Pittsburgh; 7. Houston; 8. Cleveland; 9. Cincinnati; 10. Denver; 11. Los Angeles; 12. Seattle; 13. San Diego; 14. Kansas City

NATIONAL FOOTBALL CONFERENCE

1. New Orleans; 2. San Francisco; 3. Dallas; 4. Philadelphia; 5. Washington; 6. Saint Louis; 7. New York; 8. Minnesota; 9. Green Bay; 10. Detroit; 11. Chicago; 12. Tampa Bay; 13. Los Angeles; 14. Atlanta

Para-graphs

1. 2; 1
2. 2; 4
3. October
4. September, December and November, January; August, December and November, January; 1979
5. September, December; August, December; August; September

Follow-Up Activity

1. 5; Robert Newhouse; Butch Johnson
2. 30;
3. 1979-190; 1980-200
4. 1979-75; 1980-80
5. Fewest-Butch Johnson; Most-Drew Pearson
6. 1979 was a worse year because the receivers caught fewer passes.
7. Jay Saldi; Drew Pearson

Sports Riddles

1. Chargers, 2. Broncos, 3. Oilers, 4. Buccaneers, 5. Redskins, 6. Eagles, 7. Rams, 8. Saints, 9. Steelers, 10. Packers, 11. Giants, 12. 49'ers, 13. Seahawks

What's the Meaning of All This

SOUTH EDGES NORTH, 20-17

The South All-Stars clipped the North All-Stars Saturday night in a game that was not determined until the final play.

Jack Fisher, the South's kickoff return specialist, took the opening kickoff at the 15, evaded 2 tacklers by side-stepping them at the 25, and raced the remaining 75 yards to paydirt for the South's first touchdown.

However, the North was not to be outdone. Clyde Moss took the following kickoff and sprinted down the right sideline for the North's first score. This return was a duplicate of the earlier return by the South, because it was an exact copy in terms of yards covered.

The score stood at 7–7 until Mike Lee of the North scored on a one-yard dive to make the score 13–7. James Smith's conversion attempt was true as the ball split the uprights to give the North a 14–7 advantage.

The South All-Stars covered 80 yards in 15 plays late in the second quarter. Jeff Phipps' 4-yard run and Anderson's second successful conversion was the result of this long drive. As the first half ended, both teams entered their dressing rooms in a dead-lock. The score was tied, 14–14.

Neither team scored in the third quarter. There were numerous miscues. The third quarter was plagued by penalties, costly fumbles, and interceptions.

The first 3 plays of the fourth quarter proved costly for the South team. On the initial series of downs of the final period, the South lost yardage on first and second down. Then, on third down quarterback Ron Lynn was intercepted by North linebacker Grant Jones on the South 35-yard line.

On 3 successive tries, the North squad gained only 2 yards on first down, 1 yard on second down, and 2 yards on third down. Faced with the decision to go for the first down or kick a field goal, North coach Bill Lowe chose the latter. Smith's 29-yard field goal gave the North a 17–14 edge.

However, the South proved that they could rise again. With 9 seconds left in the game, the South had 36 yards to go for the game winner. The finale was spectacular as end Tom Green caught the touchdown pass on the last play of the game. The South won the game 20–17.

Follow-Up Activity

A.	9	D.	2	G.	4
B.	5	E.	1	H.	7
C.	8	F.	3	I.	6
				J.	10

Name That Horse
Follow-Up Activity

Golf; football; rodeo; boxing; baseball; basketball; tennis; soccer; football; basketball; golf

Straight from the Horse's Mouth

1. fast gun—a jockey flown in to ride a particular horse
2. fought off a wilting attack—staying ahead of a weakening opponent
3. pulled out a head victory—won by the length of a horse's head
4. Triple Crown journey—the 3 biggest races held every year
5. victory slice—the winner's share of the total prize money
6. broke a bit sluggishly—got off to a slow start
7. appeared ready to nail—almost ready to pass
8. the top money line—the category of wagering that handles "big" bets
9. centered their mutuel attentions—placing a bet
10. mustered a brisk charge—a sudden surge of speed
11. she ran out of ground—the race ended
12. shifted into high gear—running at top speed

Example of
figurative
expressions

colorful descriptor

Example of
context clue

context clues

context clues

****
RACING
****

Ruidoso Downs

Easily Smashed in Narrow Kansas Derby Win

Ruidoso Downs, N.M.—Easily Smashed fought off a wilting attack from Runnin Barre and pulled out a head victory in the 7th running of the Kansas Derby at Ruidoso Downs.

The Kansas Derby, the first stop on the Triple Crown journey for three-year-olds, offered a gross purse of $224,740. The victory slice amounted to $76,909. The amount distributed in the finale alone was $187,657 (plus a $5,000 breeder's award).

Easily Smashed, who performed in the 400-yard Derby as a 2-1 favorite, is owned by the partnership of Carl Childs, William Leach and Sue May of Ft. Stockton, TX. Leach also trains the colt. The pilot is Jackie Martin.

The winning time of 20.09 seconds (a seasonal record) was a considerable improvement over Easy Joni Jet's top-qualifying time of 20.34. The qualifying trials, however, were run under extremely windy conditions. The conditions for the May 24 Derby finale were perfect. It was a clear, sunny afternoon, with only a slight, occasional breeze.

Although Easily Smashed qualified 10th best, Ruidoso patrons figured he was still the one to beat, and made him the choice in the finale. His big selling point was a two-length win in the trials, plus the top money line of close to $160,000.

Fans who centered their mutuel attentions on Easily Smashed in the Kansas Derby collected $6, $3.69 and $3. The son of Easy Jet out of Smash I

came out of the Derby with a perfect '81 record of three-for-three. Last year, he compiled outstanding marks of 9-2-0 from 13 outings.

Runnin Barre, ridden by Steve Treasure for Robert and Juanita Ballenger of Paoli, OK., banked $35,158 for his runner-up effort. The tote returns were $3.80 and $3.40. Easy Joni Jet owned by Louie Allen of Allen, TX., mustered a brisk charge in the final stages but had to settle for third, a neck behind Runnin Barre. The show price was $4. Easy Joni Jet carried odds of better than 9-1. The third-place paycheck amounted to $18,018.

Easily Smashed got off to a strong get-away from the rail slot and quickly assumed command. Mighty Pass Em. Easy Joni Jet and Moon Chicks quickly got into some tight quarters from the Nos. 1, 3, and 4 posts. Runnin Barre broke a bit sluggishly and bore in a bit.

Easily Smashed was clearly in charge when he was about 100 yards away from the gate, although some arguments were delivered by Native Tea, a 15-1 longshot. Just when things appeared to be in the bag for Easily Smashed, Runnin Barre shifted into high gear on the far outside. She pieced together a tremendous charge and appeared ready to nail Easily Smashed when she ran out of ground.

For Easily Smashed, the win was his first major victory since his conquest of the $250,388 Sun Country Futurity at Sunland Park in the spring of 1980.

Here's how the also-rans checked in for the Kansas Derby: 4th-Ooh Lala Lala, earning $9,448; 5th-Native Tea. $8,569; 6th-Moses Lad, $8,350; 7th-Mighty Pass Em, $8,130; 8th-El Rey Burner, $7,910; 9th-Pajaro Chick, $7,960; and 10th-Moon Chicks, $7,471.

Moon Chicks lost a stirrup during the race.

Jockey Martin sized up the victory in this way: "Easily Smashed is just a super horse. He was ahead about a length 1,000 yards away from the gate. Then we came over the hump leading onto the main track, and he kind of stumbled. I picked him up and he started running real hard. They were coming pretty hard at us in the last 100 yards.

Martin had his choice of four horses to ride in the Derby finale, and opted for Easily Smashed—despite the colt's bottom qualifying time. "Easily Smashed was good to me last year with more than $150,000 in winnings and I thought he'd run a strong race in the Derby," he explained. "In the trials, he ran against a head wind, so his time didn't bother me."

Martin's three other qualifiers were Runnin Barre, Moses Lad and Ooh Lala Lala.

Steve Treasurer, the fast gun who was imported to handle Runnin Barre, observed: "She broke in a little and I took hold. Then she came flying. I'm sure she lost a little ground at the start."

figurative
expression

Example of
colorful
descriptors and
figurative
expressions

colorful
descriptor

figurative
expression

Time Signals

Miss Thermolark Wins Champion of Champions

By Cathy Dixon

Winning for the 14th time out of her 20 career starts, Miss Thermolark took home the Champion of Champion's trophy after running the 440 yards in a brisk :21.65. The 1975 bay mare's speed has been surpassed in the Champion of Champions only by Dash For Cash who set the record with speeds of :21.17 and :21.62 the past two years.

Owned by Ronny Schliep of Sallisaw, Oklahoma, the new champion was under the training of highly respected Blane Schvaneveldt. Schvaneveldt, who had won three other races that afternoon said, "We really haven't done anything differently; it's just that this horse has always been so easy to train. We thought we had a real good shot before the race and we think she should

have an excellent shot at championship honors."

The Champion of Champions has often been a stepping-stone to the World Champion Quarter Running Horse title honor with four of the past six winners having become the world champion. If Miss Thermolark becomes the 1978 champion, she will be joining the ranks of such greats as Easy Date, Mr. Jet Moore and Dash For Cash.

At the December 23 race, Miss Thermolark broke on top and appeared to have the race won, then 27-1 longshot Native Creek showed how he earned his invitation to the prestigious race and began picking up ground. Native Creek's jockey, Richard Bickel, moved the stallion to the outside of Miss Thermolark but ran out of ground too early, finishing second by only a head.

Miss Thermolark was ridden by jockey Kenny Hart, who is second this year in number of wins, and first for the second straight year in money won. Hart said, "She really broke well, and it enabled us to get a very easy lead. I was pretty sure we had the race won. When Native Creek came up on the outside, I just waved the whip at Miss Thermolark and she held him off," Hart said.

Miss Thermolark was second in the wagering to sixth place finisher Medley Glass. Miss Thermolark returned $7.40, $4.20 and $3.80, and combined with Native Creek on a $5 exacta for $393.50. The win entitles Miss Thermolark to a starting spot in next year's Champion of Champions and the $63,750 winner's purse boosted her lifetime earnings to $441,828.

Winning for the 14th time out of her 20 career starts, Miss Thermolark took home the Champion of Champion's trophy after running the 440 yards in a brisk :21.65.

Schvaneveldt, who had won three other races that afternoon said, "We really haven't done anything differently; it's just that this horse has always been that easy to train. We thought we had a real good shot before the race and we think she should have an excellent shot at championship honors."

The Champion of Champions has often been a stepping-stone to the World Champion Quarter Running Horse title honor with four of the past six winners having become the world champion.

At the December 23 race, Miss Thermolark broke on top and appeared to have the race won, then 27-1 longshot Native Creek showed how he earned his invitation to the prestigious race and began picking up ground. Native Creek's jockey, Richard Bickel, moved the stallion to the outside of Miss Thermolark but ran out of ground too early, finishing second by only a head.

Miss Thermolark was ridden by jockey Kenny Hart, who is second this year in number of wins, and first for the second straight year in money won.

Miss Thermolark was second in the wagering to sixth place finisher Medley Glass. the win entitles Miss Thermolark to a starting spot in next year's Champion of Champions and the $63,750 winner's purse boosted her lifetime earnings to $441,828.

Follow-Up Activity

Saying from the track announcer:

All is lost that is poured into a leaky bucket.

The Hand Is Quicker than the Eye or Club

A Bibliography of Sports-Related Books

> When we gloriously forget ourselves and plunge Soul-forward, headlong, into a book's profound, Impassioned for its beauty and salt of truth—'Tis then we get the right good from a book.
>
> —*Elizabeth Barrett Browning, 1806–1861*

Using the examples presented in the activities section of this book, parents and teachers can design their own sports-related reading and writing activities. The following bibliography contains a number of books that can be adapted for these purposes. This is only a partial list and is not meant as an absolute guide. Parents and teachers are helped in choosing books for specific students by the estimate of grade level difficulty which appears at the end of each annotated reference. These are cited as being appropriate for elementary or middle students. *Elementary* refers to youngsters from the ages of 7–10, depending upon their reading strengths and interests. *Middle School* refers to students from ages 11 to 14.

For parents and teachers who wish to use books that do not appear in this bibliography, the Fry Readability Graph follows. This will help establish approximate reading difficulty levels for these materials. The graph aids in identifying books that are more consistent with readers' abilities in the elementary or middle school ranges.

However, it is worth emphasizing that *approximate* levels of reading difficulty are established through the use of these readability graphs. Most graphs like the *Fry* rely heavily on syllable count and the number of sentences per passage as a means of determining how hard something may be for a particular age student to read. But there are many more factors involved in making these judgments. The following list provides some additional features of written material that cause it to be more or less difficult to read but are seldom given ample consideration by those who compile the standards for measuring reading difficulty:

1. Word length
2. Percentage of different words
3. Sentence length
4. Personal references
5. Number of difficult words according to word lists
6. Density and unusualness of the facts
7. Interrelationship of ideas
8. Organization of the material
9. Concept load—abstractness of the words
10. Interest and purpose of the reader

At best, graphs offer a "thumbnail" sketch of whether or not a certain book can be read and understood by students who appear to be reading within a given range; at their worst they oversimplify the process of evaluating reading difficulty and may underestimate or overestimate the appropriateness of using specific materials.

GRAPH FOR ESTIMATING READABILITY—EXTENDED*

by Edward Fry, Rutgers University Reading Center, New Brunswick, N.J. 08904

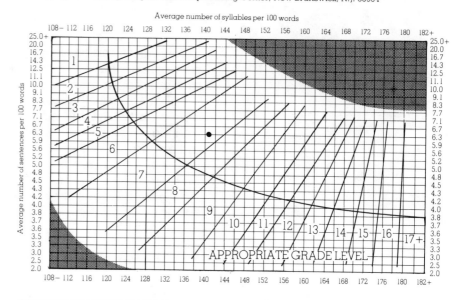

EXPANDED DIRECTIONS FOR WORKING READABILITY GRAPH

1. Randomly select three (3) sample passages and count out exactly 100 words each, beginning with the beginning of a sentence. Do count proper nouns, initializations, and numerals.
2. Count the number of sentences in the hundred words, estimating length of the fraction of the last sentence to the nearest one-tenth.
3. Count the total number of syllables in the 100-word passage. If you don't have a hand counter available, an easy way is to simply put a mark above every syllable in each word, then when you get to the end of the passage, count the number of marks and add 100. Small calculators can also be used as counters by pushing numeral 1, then push the + sign for each word or syllable when counting.
4. Enter graph with average sentence length and average number of syllables; plot dot where the two lines intersect. Area where dot is plotted will give you the approximate grade level.
5. If a great deal of variability is found in syllable count or sentence count, putting more samples into the average is desirable.
6. A word is defined as a group of symbols with a space on either side; thus, *Joe*, *IRA*, *1945*, and *&* are each one word.
7. A syllable is defined as a phonetic syllable. Generally, there are as many syllables as vowel sounds. For example, *stopped* is one syllable and *wanted* is two syllables. When counting syllables for numerals and initializations, count one syllable for each symbol. For example, *1945* is four syllables, *IRA* is three syllables, and *&* is one syllable.

NOTE: This "extended graph" does not outmode or render the earlier (1968) version inoperative or inaccurate; it is an extension. (REPRODUCTION PERMITTED—NO COPYRIGHT)

---

*Assessing approximate levels of grade-level reading difficulty using the *Fry Readability Graph* (*Journal of Reading*, 21, December 1977, 242–52).

E=Elementary

M=Middle School

Baseball

Mel Cebulash, *Baseball Players Do Amazing Things* (New York: Random House, 1973), 69 pp.
A collection of true stories about some of the most colorful players in big-league baseball history. Included are the more unusual antics demonstrated by such players as Babe Ruth, Willie Mays, Stan Musial, Dizzy Dean, and others. The large print, the controlled vocabulary, and the short, 2–3 page chapters make this book most appropriate for the early elementary reader. Teachers should find the author's abundant use of sight words useful in providing reinforcement for learning these terms. [E]

R. Guidry, and P. Golenbuck, *Guidry* (New York: Avon Books, 1980), 173 pp.
An intriguing biographical sketch of Ron Guidry who, at the onset of his baseball career, was told by George Steinbrenner that he would never be able to pitch in the major leagues. The diverse vocabulary makes this book most appropriate for the able as well as the less able junior high or high school student. Teachers should find this book useful when teaching students such study skills as identifying main ideas, locating supporting details, and outlining. [M]

H. Liss, and J. Devancy, *The Pocket Book of Baseball* (New York: Pocket Books, 1981), 246 pp.
This book presents team-by-team analysis of the American League and includes feature stories on George Brett, Rick Cerone, Mike Schmidt, Billy Martin, and Steve Garvey. Also included are 16 pages of action photos. The detailed analysis of each team may be useful in developing questions that measure students' inferential comprehension as well as their ability to distinguish cause and effect relationships. Teachers should find the feature stories good examples of descriptive writing that provide students an opportunity to express their opinions regarding the author's portrayal of these baseball teams and superstars. The book also includes diagrams of batting statistics for each individual player and club. These are useful in providing students experience reading charts and graphs. [M]

Bill Mazer, *Bill Mazer's Baseball Trivia* (New York: Warner Books, Inc., 1981), 188 pp.
This pocket book presents 3–4-paragraph passages covering certain persons or events in baseball including a number of trivia items. Each passage is followed by a "Quickie Quiz." The text provides excellent examples of paragraph organization, i.e., topic sentences and supporting details which will prove beneficial when teaching such study skills as outlining, identifying main ideas, and locating supporting details. Teachers should find this book an excellent source for encouraging recall and literal comprehension. [M]

Joseph McBride, *The Complete Guide to Baseball Slang* (New York: Warner Books, Inc., 1980), 288 pp.
This book contains the various origins and definitions of slang terms used in baseball and depicts players' nicknames as well. A major

attraction of the work is the general index, which teachers may find useful when teaching reference skills, i.e., locating and using various sections of a book. Teachers may also find this book helpful in developing students' understanding of synonyms and antonyms. [M]

John R. Tunis, *The Kid Comes Back* (New York: Bantam Books, 1977), 183 pp.

A story of a baseball player who returns from war. His injured leg causes some pessimism among his teammates and fans. This thrilling novel depicts the pain, struggle, and determination experienced by the returning soldier, culminating in a thrilling victory, both for the kid and his team. The book's high interest level combined with a relatively easy vocabulary makes it an excellent vehicle to motivate the less able reader. Teachers should find the vast amount of dialog contained in the book useful in demonstrating the relationship between spoken and written language. [M]

John R. Tunis, *World Series* (New York: Bantam Books, 1977), 195 pp.

Presents an inside view of a baseball player's perspective of the game prior to, during, and after his participation in the World Series. Teachers should find this book an excellent means to motivate the avid baseball fan to read. Much of the book is written in the first person and teachers will find this work useful as a tool for developing youngsters' vocabulary and language experiences. [M]

Basketball

D. Barnett, *Inside Basketball* (Chicago: Contemporary Books, Inc., 1971), 87 pp.

This book, printed in large type, introduces the beginning "hoop" enthusiast to the fundamentals of basketball. Written by former New York Knickerbocker Dick Barnett, this book suggests appropriate methods for developing and executing specific maneuvers in basketball such as dribbling, passing, rebounding, and shooting. Each chapter includes action photographs illustrating various moves. This provides clarity for the less able reader. Teachers may want to use the picture illustrations as topics for creative writing activities by having students write short paragraphs explaining the move pictured. [M]

M. Bell, *The Legend of Dr. J* (New York: New American Library, 1976).

This book profiles the basketball career of "Dr. J," (Julius Erving), from his first quarter as a substitute player for the Roosevelt High Bulls to his trade to Philadelphia. The book's high-interest level, along with its relatively simple vocabulary, may attract the able fifth- or sixth-grade reader, as well as older students who have reading problems. [M]

G. Goodrich, and R. Levin, *Winning Basketball* (Chicago: Contemporary Books, 1976), 138 pp.

Written by former UCLA guard Gail Goodrich, this book presents guidelines for developing winning strategies in basketball. Included are tips on how wit and intelligence can compensate for inferior strength and height and suggestions on how to prepare physically for a game. The author provides a word of warning to those considering a career in pro basketball, suggesting a more realistic approach to setting goals. Easy-to-read and fully illustrated, middle school teachers will find this book most appropriate for the less able reader interested in basketball. [M]

Z. Hollander, ed., *The Complete Handbook of Pro Basketball* (New York: New American Library, 1981), 319 pp.
Presents complete rosters for all 23 NBA teams, including individual and team profiles, photographs, and statistics. In addition, a list of all-time NBA records is provided, as well as an official 1981–82 schedule. Students having sufficient experiential background in basketball will find this book a useful source of information. Teachers may find the 2-paragraph profiles useful in creating comprehension activities such as matching the players with their profile, comparing the statistics of individuals and teams, or in constructing various playing card games requiring players to form "books" on team members. [M]

Z. Hollander, ed., *The NBA's Official Encyclopedia of Pro Basketball* (New York: New American Library, 1981), 532 pp.
Presenting a historical profile of basketball, the information contained in this book spans the game from its conception in 1896 to the present. Included in this volume are numerous pieces of basketball trivia such as Chuck Conners' (The Rifleman) career with the Boston Celtics in 1947, as well as providing complete profiles of basketball's greats such as Julius "Dr. J" Erving, Kareem Abdul-Jabbar, and Larry Bird. Also included are discussions of all the all-star games, the Basketball Hall of Fame Roster, and the official NBA rules. Organized on the same format as an encyclopedia, teachers may find this book an excellent means of introducing students to the use of reference materials. [M]

N. Lieberman, *Basketball My Way* (New York: Charles Scribner's Sons, 1982), 139 pp.
Written by Nancy Lieberman, the first female to play in an all-male summer professional basketball league, this book provides middle and high school age girls interested in the game detailed discussions concerning offensive and defensive techniques and also includes official basketball rules for both men and women. Young women less interested in playing will find the sections featuring nutrition, weight watching, and muscle toning of interest. Complete with a detailed glossary of basketball-related terms, this book provides teachers an excellent source of vocabulary enrichment in a well-written and interesting context. [M]

G. L. Miller, *Official's Manual in Basketball* (New York: Leisure Press, 1981), 79 pp.
Presents official NBA rules and suggested guidelines for officiating basketball. This manual, complete with instructions, provides not only game rules, but also illustrations of various fouls and infractions. Also, the appropriate positioning of officials during the course of a game is explained. With its stress on rules, this book could be an excellent source for developing literal reading comprehension. [M]

B. Russell, and B. Taylor, *Second Wind* (New York: Ballantine Books, 1979), 303 pp.
Presents the memoirs of Bill Russell, former center for the Boston Celtics, sketching Russell's life from the time he was 7 to his legendary years in the NBA. Adding to this book's appeal are Russell's humorous anecdotes. Teachers wanting to encourage reading for pleasure in the classroom will find their job made easier as a result of having *Second Wind* on their bookshelves. [M]

C. Wielgus, and A. Wolf, *The In-Your-Face Basketball Book* (New York: Everest House, 1980), 186 pp.
Each chapter suggests how one should modify his/her behavior to survive a street game. The book provides readers with such tips as appropriate language for street-ball players, unique scoring procedures, violations, and instructions on how to get into a game and includes numerous photographs of make-shift basketball courts around the United States. The book also suggests various games appropriate for 1–5 players as well as a selection describing unique playing characteristics of various ethnic groups and cultures. For the serious street "hoop shooter," a section entitled "Forbidden Fundamentals" is provided. This book will prove to be a great motivator for the reluctant reader. Teachers may find the section on terminology a fine source for vocabulary development activities. [M]

R. Youngman, *Officiating Basketball* (Chicago: Contemporary Books, Inc., 1978), 138 pp.
Presents guidelines for refereeing basketball. Teachers will find this book an excellent source for encouraging students to read for details and cause-effect relationships. [M]

Football

Clary Anderson, *The Young Sportsman's Guide to Football* (New York: Thomas Nelson and Sons, 1963), 92 pp.
Presents the fundamentals of football through diagrams and illustrations. The text is organized in small units, each consisting of short passages. These units are followed by diagrams illustrating fundamentals discussed in the text. Teachers should find the discussion of fundamentals useful when teaching students to identify main ideas and locate supporting details. Students might be asked to draw their own diagrams illustrating what they understand to be the main idea of each unit. [M]

Robert J. Antonacci, and Jene Barr, *Football For Young Champions*, illus. by Rus Anderson (New York: McGraw-Hill Book Co., Inc., 1958), 159 pp.
Discusses rules, gives history of the game, and describes training equipment. Teachers may find the discussion of the game's history useful in developing exercises for literal recall, i.e., specific information such as names, dates, places, and events. [M]

Marshall Burchard, and Sue Burchard, *Sports Heroes: O. J. Simpson* (New York: G. P. Putnam and Sons, 1975), 58 pp.
Discusses the life and football career of O.J. Simpson. Each chapter contains black and white photo illustrations of "the Juice" in action. The high interest level of this book should prove useful as a means of motivating reluctant readers. The accompanying action photos of Simpson should stimulate even the least interested reader to enthusiastically peruse the pages of this book. [M]

Sue Burchard, *Tony Dorsett* (New York: Harcourt, Brace, and Jovanovich, 1978), 64 pp.
A biographical outline of Dorsett's life, from his childhood through his present superstar status with the Dallas Cowboys. Teachers may want to print various events in Dorsett's life on cards, asking students to sequence them in the order of their occurrence. [E]

Mel Cebulash, *Football Players Do Amazing Things* (New York: Random House, 1975), 64 pp.
Presents some of football's most colorful players and their stories of unusual and often funny situations. The humorous topics, combined with a vocabulary of limited difficulty, should serve to attract the able middle school reader as well as the older student experiencing some reading difficulty. [M]

Arthur Daley, *Pro Football's Hall of Fame* (New York: Quadrangle Books, 1963), 248 pp.
Presents, in chronological order, the lives and football careers of the 17 men selected as the first entrants into the professional football Hall of Fame. Students interested in pro football may find this work an excellent source of information for writing themes and essays on famous personalities. [M]

Dick Fishel, and Red Smith, *Terry and Bunky Play Football* (New York: G. P. Putnam and Sons, 1945), 80 pp.
Presented in a simple storybook form, the authors use the adventures of Terry and Bunky to describe the basic rules and techniques of football. Students will enjoy reading the humorous conversations between Terry and Bunky. Elementary. teachers will find this type of book useful in demonstrating the relationship between spoken and written language to beginning readers. [E]

Leonard Kessler, *Super Bowl* (Los Angeles: Greenwillow, 1976).
This book makes use of a child's fantasy when the "Animal Champs" challenge the "Super Birds" in football's biggest game, the Super Bowl. Teachers should find the author's abundant use of sight words useful in developing early readers' sight-word recognition skills in context. [E]

Vince Lombardi, and W. C. Hering, *Run to Daylight!* (Englewood Cliffs, NJ: Prentice-Hall, Inc., 1963), 300 pp.
Describes 7 days in the life of Vince Lombardi, using word and picture stories. This book presents the behind-the-scene workings of a pro football team. The book may serve to motivate students who share a basic love of the game to read. Teachers should find the vocabulary level suitable for the more capable sixth-grade reader, as well as the high school student having marginal reading difficulties. [M]

Joseph Olgin, *Illustrated Football Dictionary For Young People* (Englewood Cliffs, NJ: Prentice-Hall, Inc., 1975), 112 pp.
Defines a wide range of terms used in football. Teachers should find this book useful in developing students' reference skills. Youngsters are attracted to the text's format and illustrations and find it more appealing than the standard dictionary. [E]

John Thorn, *Pro Football's Ten Greatest Games* (New York: Four Winds Press, 1981), 208 pp.
Presents the 10 greatest games (according to the author) played in the National Football League. The first game describes action between the New York Giants and the Chicago Bears in 1933. The book culminates with the celebrated Washington Redskins-Dallas Cowboy match of 1979. The pages in between are filled with an assortment of colorful expressions and terminology, making it an excellent source for vocabulary or language enrichment. [M]

Golf   Dick Aultman, *101 Ways to Win at Golf* (Norwalk, CT: Golf Digest/ Tennis, Inc., 1980), 192 pp.

Referred to as a primer in golf, this book presents the basic fundamentals of the game. The subject matter, combined with a simple, easy-to-read vocabulary, makes it most appropriate for the able third-grade reader as well as the older reader having marginal reading difficulties. Because of the book's carefully controlled vocabulary, teachers will discover it to be an excellent means of reinforcing youngsters' recognition of sight words in context. In addition, teachers may develop comprehension activities focusing on cause and effect relationships by exploring the factors behind the fundamentals discussed, i.e., What do you think would happen if your grip on the club was not tight enough? Why do you think the author says to keep your eyes on the ball?, etc. [M]

W. T. Gallwey, *The Inner Game of Golf* (New York: Random House, 1981), 207 pp.

This book deals with the mental aspects of golf, i.e., concentration, emotions, anxiety, etc., as opposed to the mechanics of the game. The author believes that these fundamentals, referred to as the "Inner Game," will not only serve to reduce players' handicaps on the golf course, but can serve to reduce one's "handicap" in life as well. Teachers should find the abundance of base words and suffixes associated with golf useful in developing students' word-building skills, e.g., breaking, putting, chipping. [M]

Jack Nicklaus, *Jack Nicklaus' Lesson Tee* (New York: Simon and Schuster, 1977), 157 pp.

Written and illustrated in comic book form, this book should prove useful as a means of motivating reluctant readers. Each fundamental is presented and illustrated in a series of colored frames with captioned explanations. The illustrations should benefit the less able reader in clarifying the text. [M]

Jack Nicklaus, *Play Better Golf* (New York: Pocket Books, 1981).

This pocket book is written for the avid golfer who would like to reduce his/her score without taking lessons. The author has creatively organized the book into a series of frames, each graphically illustrating a particular fundamental, accompanied by a 2-paragraph captioned explanation. The less able fourth- and fifth-grade reader will find the vocabulary manageable. The accompanying illustrations will also serve to clarify the text for students with marginal reading problems. [E]

Jack Nicklaus, and Ken Bowden, *Play Better Golf, The Swing From A-Z* (New York: Pocket Books, 1980), 200 pp.

This pocket book presents step-by-step instructions in comic strip form on how to improve your swing. The frames sequentially illustrate a particular type of swing and are accompanied by easy-to-read explanations in caption form. Teachers will find the comic strip format a unique means of motivating the reluctant reader. The abundant use of compound words associated with golf, for example, backswing, clubhead, backspin, downswing, flagstick, etc., may prove useful in developing beginning readers' word building skills. [E]

PGA Communications Department, *Official PGA Tour Media Guide* (New York: Workman Publishing Co., Inc., 1980), 241 pp.

Presents the history and background of the PGA Tour, as well as a look at how the organization operates. This book includes extensive biographical information of leading players and shorter sketches of other prominent personalities in golf. The book contains a wealth of records, statistics, facts, and figures describing the current status of each player. Teachers will find the book's abundant use of charts and graphs an excellent means of providing students experience in reading this type of material, in a context of interest to the golf enthusiast. The short biographical sketches should prove useful when teaching students skills in identifying main ideas, locating supporting details, and outlining. The book may also prove beneficial as a source of information for writing themes and essays. [M]

Charles Price, and Editors of *Sports Illustrated, Sports Illustrated Golf* (Philadelphia, PA: J. B. Lippincott Co., 1970).
This book is written for the novice golfer. The authors describe, in understandable terms, different types of clubs and their uses. Included are numerous photographs illustrating the proper stance, grip, and various type of swings. A major highlight of this book is the glossary of golf terms which teachers may find useful in developing students' reference skills as well as broadening their reading vocabularies. The numerous photo illustrations can serve to clarify the text for students having marginal reading difficulties. [M]

Gymnastics

P. Akroyd, *Skills and Tactics of Gymnastics* (New York: Arco Publishing Co., 1980), 152 pp.
This book presents sequenced frames illustrating basic gymnastic routines accompanied by brief explanations. Intended to serve as an introduction to the sport, the author offers the novice gymnast practical advice concerning initial training techniques, precautionary measures, and tips on preparing for competition. Other features include color photographs of noted gymnasts such as Nadia Comaneci, diagrams of equipment, exercises, and body positions. Also included is a complete glossary of terms and an index. This work may be useful for developing sequencing activities such as matching diagrams with their corresponding instructions. Likewise, the glossary of terms and the index may prove interesting content for developing students' reference skills. [M]

J. Coulton, *Women's Gymnastics* (West Yorkshire, England: EP Publishing Ltd., 1977), 116 pp.
The purpose of this paperback is to provide gymnasts with instructions for basic gymnastic exercises. With the aid of over 300 sequentially organized photographs and numerous diagrams, the reader is provided examples of each body position and movement accompanied by brief and clearly written explanations. This type of book will be beneficial when teaching youngsters to follow written directions. [M]

M. Engle, S. Engle, and R. Hanson, *Gymnastics: The New Era* (New York: Grosset and Dunlap, 1980), 96 pp.
Packed with black and white action photographs, this paperback contains sections on the history of gymnastics, the American era, equipment and events, methods for scoring and judging, and a chapter outlining how to get started in the sport. Teachers may find the chapters describing a gymnast's daily routine and practice schedules excellent vehicles for teaching chronological order and sequence of events. Youngsters interested in this popular sport should enjoy reading this book. [E–M]

R. Ito, and C. Dolney, *Mastering Women's Gymnastics* (Chicago: Contemporary Books, Inc., 1978), 160 pp.
Written primarily for the novice gymnast, this paperback presents guidelines for training and exercising, arranged to parallel a typical workout. Clearly organized with easy-to-follow instructions, this book should serve as a useful source for teaching sequential comprehension. The first chapter, written in outline form, is an excellent example for teaching students to locate main ideas and supporting details. [M]

J. Krementz, *A Very Young Gymnast* (New York: Alfred A. Knopf, Inc., 1980), 128 pp.
Written in the first person, this book describes the life of a 10-year-old gymnast. Accompanying the text are excellent black and white photographs. The print is set in large type and the author uses simple sentence structures to discuss the demanding life of gymnastic competition. Teachers should find this volume a useful source for such comprehension skills as cause and effect and sequence of events. [E]

R. Neil, *The Official Cheerleader's Handbook* (New York: Simon and Schuster, 1979).
Intended as a guide for young women interested in applying their gymnastic skills to cheerleading, this work offers instructions pertaining to exercise, gymnastic stunts, and various types of cheers. Accompanying each series of instructions are black and white action photographs illustrating each maneuver described. Additional features include a brief history of cheerleading, ideas for fund raising, and guidelines for understanding organized sports. Teachers wanting to motivate students to read for pleasure should find this a pertinent guide for middle school girls. [M]

F. Ryan, *Gymnastics for Girls* (New York: Penguin Books, 1976), 433 pp.
Written by a sports enthusiast who holds a Ph.D. in psychology, this book is a comprehensive guide for young gymnasts. Illustrated with action photographs of junior high girls performing the described movements, the book explains basic exercises in terms that are understandable to the layperson. The brevity of the paragraphs provides an excellent source for developing vocabulary and word recognition in context. [M]

E. Wachtel, and N. C. Looken, *Girls' Gymnastics* (New York: Sterling Publishing Co., 1979), 186 pp.
Illustrated with black and white photographs, this work describes in simple text the basics of girls' gymnastics. The instructions for executing gymnastic movements are brief and will serve to attract the reluctant reader. The short explanatory paragraphs should also allow the older, less able reader an opportunity to read material written at an appropriate level of difficulty and corresponding to specific interests. [M]

J. Wiley, *Women's Gymnastics* (Mountain View, CA: Anderson World, Inc., 1980), 176 pp.
Written primarily for young women interested in gymnastics, this paperback offers information on proper clothing and equipment, basic conditioning techniques, and the fundamentals of various routines. Also included are the official rules of competition, an outline of the criteria generally followed by judges, and a complete roster of gymnastic organizations around the country. Students lacking sufficient

experience in gymnastics may find the specialized vocabulary difficult to read; however, those more familiar with the sport will find the instructions clearly written and easy to follow. [M]

Horsemanship

G. Henschel, *A Horseman's Handbook: Basic Riding Explained* (New York: Arco Publishing Co., Inc., 1980).
This book describes the basic elements of horsemanship, including instructions for selecting and caring for horses. It contains colorful photographs to illustrate various facets of horsemanship. This book lends itself to teaching students the importance of sequence. The text contains specialized vocabulary related to the sport, and readers encounter many context clues to aid their understanding. The appendix contains a list of addresses of numerous riding associations. [M]

J. Krementz, *A Very Young Rider* (New York: Alfred A. Knopf, 1979).
The text is written in an easy-to-read first person narrative style and requires no prior knowledge of horsemanship to be understandable. Most terms and expressions are well-explained. The print is large and each page contains small amounts of textual material accompanied by photographic illustrations. This book is useful for introducing students to new vocabulary in a meaningful context. The descriptions of the rider's training and her daily routine in caring for her horse are helpful for teaching students the importance of sequence. [E]

R. Owen, *Learning to Ride* (New York: Arco Publishing Co., 1981), 111 pp.
Aimed at young, novice riders, this book describes the basic elements of horsemanship. While the vocabulary may prove difficult for students lacking experiential background in equestrian sports, the brief 1–2 page chapters prove motivating for reluctant readers who know something about horses. [M]

J. Starkey, ed., *Horse Sense: Buying and Looking after Your First Horse* (New York: Sterling Publishing Co., 1981).
This hardbound book offers practical advice in clear, concise language. Step-by-step illustrations and colorful photographs will catch the attention of youngsters and assist in explaining certain technical terms, procedures, and use of equipment. [M]

M. A. Stoneridge, *A Horse of Your Own* (Garden City, NY: Doubleday & Co., Inc., 1980), 536 pp.
This book is a basic encyclopedia guide to the equestrian world. The various breeds and types of horses are described; possible stabling arrangements are discussed. Specific topics such as proper feeding, grooming equipment, clothing, breeding, and training for show are presented in some detail. Because of the wide variety of information contained in this book, teachers may find it useful for providing students practice in locating ideas and supporting details or sequencing and following directions. [M]

Martial Arts

Bong Soo Han, *Hapkido, Korean Art of Self-defense* (Burbank, CA: Ohara Publications, Inc., 1980), 192 pp.
Presents the history and philosophy of Hapkido, followed by 150 pages of captioned photos and step-by-step instructions. The limited amount of text combined with numerous pages of action photos serve to attract students who would otherwise generally avoid reading. [M]

Joe Hyams, *Playboys Book of Practical Self-defense* (Chicago: Playboy Press, 1981), 152 pp.
Pesents a number of practical ways of self-defense. Each technique is illustrated by a series of sequenced photos with simple instructions in caption form. Teachers may find this type of book useful when teaching students to follow written directions. Students might be asked to demonstrate a technique, step by step, or to illustrate a technique on paper, providing sequential instructions. [M]

Willy Lin, *T'ien Shan P'ai Kung Fo* (Burbank, CA: Ohara Publications, Inc., 1976), 160 pp.
This work is aimed at the novice and presents an introduction to the art of T'ien Shan P'ai. The author begins by presenting operational definitions of terms used in the book, e.g., strike, adjust, half-extended, block, etc. Teachers may find this book a helpful resource for teaching word recognition using context clues. [M]

Masutatsu Ogama, *The Kyokushin Way* (Tokyo: Japan Publications, Inc., 1979), 112 pp.
This book presents the story of one of Japan's most noted authorities in the martial arts, Masutatsu Ogama. The book discusses mental attitude and discipline which, in the author's opinion, are significant to developing any skill, but particularly the skill of karate. Each chapter has a one-word title whose definition is applied to developing the skills of karate. Teachers should find the content of this book unique. It is useful in demonstrating to young people the elements of success. Teachers will discover that the chapters' titles themselves contribute to students' vocabulary development, e.g., Aspirations, Diligence, Courage, Success, etc. [M]

Bruce Tegner, *Stick-fighting: Self-defense* (Ventura, CA: Thor Publishing Co., 1979), 127 pp.
Presents a series of practical techniques for self-defense using a stick. The book contains a section of approaches for women as well as a unit on self-defense for the disabled. Each chapter contains sequential photographic illustrations of a particular technique, followed by a brief, 4–5 sentence explanation. The less able elementary reader may find the limited amount of text and the abundance of action photos interesting. [M]

Bruce Tegner, and Alice McGrath, *Self-Defense for Your Child* (Ventura, CA: Thor Publishing Co., 1976), 127 pp.
Presents a fully illustrated, clearly explained, practical course in self-defense. The techniques discussed are geared toward children between 6–10 years of age. The vocabulary should pose no problem for the able third- or fourth-grade student. [E]

Jay T. Will, *Advanced Kenpo Karate* (Hollywood, CA: Unique Publications, 1980), 115 pp.
Discusses and illustrates some of the more sophisticated aspects of the art. Photographic illustrations of techniques make up a large portion of each chapter. Each photograph is sequentially presented and captioned. The less able reader may be attracted to this particular book because it presents a sophisticated topic, mostly through pictures, followed by a limited amount of text. Teachers should find this work an excellent means of attracting students less interested in reading. [M]

Physical Fitness and Running

J. Davis, *Garfield Gains Weight* (New York: Ballantine Books, 1980), unpaginated.
This book presents the comic strip character Garfield the Cat who is portrayed as being very unfit and out of shape. Garfield's physical condition is humorously attributed to his sleeping late, inappropriate eating habits, and lack of exercise. As a result, Garfield is grouchy, his "stomach finally outgrows his legs," and he has to go visit the vet. Young readers will find this book enjoyable and easy to read. Teachers may want to point out the implied cause-effect relationships between Garfield's bad habits and his poor physical condition. [E]

J. Davis, *Garfield Weighs In* (New York: Ballantine Books, 1982), unpaginated.
This book provides a humorous view of proper exercise, nutrition, and other topics pertaining to health. An example of the author's humorous use of figurative language is, "I'm not overweight, I'm undertall." [E]

J. F. Fixx, *The Complete Book of Running.* (New York: Random House, 1977), 306 pp.
This volume covers every aspect of running, from advice to children to guidelines for heart attack victims. Other features include a complete roster of addresses where recommended equipment may be purchased as well as a bibliography of selected readings. Organized much like an encyclopedia, teachers will find this book an excellent source for teaching students study skills and use of reference materials. [M]

A. Kiemal, *I'm Running to Win* (Wheaton, IL: Tyndale House Publishers, Inc., 1981), 169 pp.
Presents the daily journal of a 34-year-old woman who decided to prepare for the Boston Marathon although she had never run before. Reluctant readers interested in long distance running will be attracted to this high interest, low vocabulary book. Teachers may find the book useful as a means of initiating students' journal writing. [M]

M. Liquori, and J. L. Parker, *Real Running* (New York: Wideview Books, 1982), 166 pp.
This book presents guidelines for training techniques, psychological strategies, and racing tactics for the competitive runner. Each of the 6 chapters focuses on a particular dimension of competitive running. Teachers will find the section on different categories of runners beneficial in teaching categorizing skills. The charts and graphs included in this book are excellent sources for practicing content area reading skills. [M]

D. Wielenga, *NFL Family Fitness Guide.* (New York: A National Football League Book, 1981), 126 pp.
Presents guidelines for physical fitness appropriate to all members of the family, regardless of age. This book contains discussions on nutrition and practical exercises for all ages and suggests various recreational sports that can promote an individual's physical fitness most effectively. [M]

Soccer

P. Gardner, and P. Woosmaunt, *Soccer, Sports Illustrated* (New York: J. P. Lippincott Co., 1972), 95 pp.
Describes various skills involved in controlling the ball without using the hands. Line drawings and action photographs accompany each discussion. These illustrations detail such skills as kicking, receiving, heading, and dribbling. Also included are the official rules governing Ameri-

can soccer. The book's use of subtitles followed by brief paragraphs provides excellent examples of main ideas and supporting details and may be used as a basis for creating activities and instruction. [M]

D. Kowet, *The Soccer Book* (New York: Random House, 1978), 156 pp.
Divided into 3 parts, this volume presents soccer from a historical perspective. It includes photographs and brief profiles of a few of soccer's most outstanding players. Also presented are several of soccer's most noteworthy contests and World Cup championships. Descriptions include the astonishing upset of West Germany over Hungary in 1954, and the 1958 World Cup Tournament when Brazil survived undefeated and introduced the young 17-year-old phenomena Pele. The remaining sections present information detailing skill development, strategies, and appropriate equipment. Also included is a complete index which teachers may find useful in providing students practice in locating specific information. The book's high interest level, large, easy-to-read print, and its abundant use of action photographs should serve to attract reluctant readers interested in soccer. [M]

A. Miller, and N. Wingert, *Winning Soccer* (Chicago: Contemporary Books, Inc., 1975), 189 pp.
A comprehensive instructional manual, this book presents the basic skills of soccer. Each chapter describes a particular skill such as dribbling, passing, heading, shooting, and kicking, followed by suggested techniques for developing that skill. In addition, the author, a former goalkeeper for the Philadelphia Atoms, has included a section on game strategies in which he discusses a few "tricks of the game." The book contains brief descriptive paragraphs students can use to practice skimming and scanning for information. [M]

B. Moffat, *The Basic Soccer Guide* (Mountain View, CA: Anderson World, Inc., 1975; 1981), 143 pp.
Divided into 3 parts, this book presents the basic skills of soccer, winning strategies, and specific safety precautions. In addition, the author suggests practical methods for players to prepare themselves physically for the game. Also included are photographs and diagrams illustrating basic formations and tactics. Teachers will find the complete glossary of soccer terms a useful source for teaching students to recognize figurative language. The book also provides students practice in the use of reference material. [M]

G. Sullivan, ed., *Soccer Rules Illustrated* (New York: Simon and Schuster, 1981), 96 pp.
This paperback lists the official rules of soccer in easy-to-read large print and is supplemented with action photos and drawings. The rules themselves provide an excellent vehicle for developing students' literal comprehension as well as sequencing skills. [M]

Tennis

S. A. Burchard, *Sports Star: John McEnroe* (New York: Harcourt, Brace, 1977), 80 pp.
This colorfully illustrated book presents an unusually honest biography of one of the world's greatest tennis players. Due to its high interest content, this book may prove beneficial in motivating young children to read for pleasure. [E–M]

Charles Coombs, *Be a Winner in Tennis* (New York: Morrow, 1975), 128 pp.
Presents a beginner's guide to tennis, describing various techniques. The author incorporates many diagrams and photographs illustrating the various strategies discussed. The organization of the book makes it an ideal tool to provide practice recognizing sequential organization of print and new vocabulary. The book also provides practice in reading and interpreting diagrams. [E–M]

Allison Danzig, and P. Schwed, *The Fireside Book of Tennis* (New York: Simon and Schuster, 1972), 1,043 pp.
Originally published in popular magazines, the articles which make up the content of this book focus on great matches, general tennis, tennis history, and superstars. The book is illustrated with many action photos. Due to the book's wide range of reading levels, it may prove useful in providing the older, less able reader interesting material that can be read with ease. [E–M]

Paul Deegan, *Tennis: Service and Returning Service* (Mankato, MN: Creative Education, 1976), 32 pp.
Geared toward the young athlete (ages 8–12), this book focuses on the basics of the serve and the return of service. The book's content and organization provide an excellent resource for developing vocabulary, as well as practice in outlining and sequencing written material. The content of the book may also prove beneficial in developing youngsters' understanding of cause and effect relationships. [E]

Dick Gradlee, *Instant Tennis: A New Approach to the Game Based on the Coordination Rhythm and Timing of Champions* (New York: Devin-Adair, 1962), 107 pp.
Presents various methods of serving used by many champion tennis players. The author describes and illustrates various methods of serving in detail. Following each lesson, a summary chart is presented summarizing the steps discussed in that chapter. The book may be useful in developing recognition of sequential organization as well as providing youngsters experience in reading charts and graphs in a context which is meaningful to the tennis enthusiast. [M]

Rod Laver, Berry Tarshis, and Roy Emerson, *Tennis for the Bloody Fun of It* (Chicago: Quatrangle, 1976), 158 pp.
Presents various aspects of the sport of tennis: etiquette, equipment, conditioning, strategy, strokes, and the psychology of the game. The book is instructional in nature but approaches the subject from the perspective of having fun while learning the fundamentals of tennis. The illustrative photographs of Laver demonstrate special techniques for the left-handed player. The organization of the content provides an excellent base for instruction in determining main ideas and supporting details as well as introducing new vocabulary. [M]

Marion Meade, *Women in Sports: Tennis* (New York: Harvey Publishing Co., 1975), 78 pp.
Rosie Casals, Billie Jean King, and Margaret Court are a few of the featured personalities in this collection of biographies. This book may be useful in getting young women who are interested in sports to read for pleasure. The content of the book is useful in developing recognition of similarities and contrasts, a skill which will strengthen comprehension. [M]

Tony Mottram, *Play Better Tennis* (New York: Arco Publishing Co., 1971), 127 pp.
Presents penny-arcade type sequence photographs of Evonne Goolagong Cawley, John Newcombe, and other tennis stars demonstrating the basic skills of tennis. By flipping the pages rapidly, the reader is able to see the final result when each skill is applied. The format of the book provides an excellent demonstration of what supporting details are and the importance of sequential comprehension. The book might also be used as a source for developing outlining activities. [E]